MUSICALLY ENGAGED *Seniors*

40 SESSION PLANS *and* RESOURCES *for a* VIBRANT MUSIC THERAPY PROGRAM

Meredith Faith Hamons, MT-BC

WHELK & WATERS PUBLISHING

Musically Engaged Seniors
© 2013 Meredith Faith Hamons
Published by:
Whelk and Waters Publishing

Book design by TLC Graphics, www.TLCGraphics.com
Cover: Chelsea Shaw; Interior: Lisa Von De Linde

Printed in the U.S.A.

ISBN-13: 978-0615896281
ISBN-10: 0615896286

Acknowledgements

Special thanks to Christy, Brigette, and Cathy for their
editing prowess and encouragement.

Endless thanks and love to my dear husband,
Christopher, who is a constant support and encouragement
and who worked to make sure I had the time and space
to complete this project.

TABLE OF CONTENTS

Laying the Groundwork

PART ONE

INTRODUCTION

It has been a dream of mine since high school to work with seniors as a music therapist. That dream came to fruition in the fall of 2010 when I founded my own company and launched the "Songs and Seniors" program as one of the core offerings of North Austin Music Therapy. Despite the on going recession and endless budget issues in long-term health and nursing care, the program grew and now serves seniors all across the greater Austin area in independent living communities, assisted living communities, memory care units, healthcare and nursing centers, rehabilitation facilities, and day programs. I couldn't enjoy my job more and am excited to see how the program will continue to grow and expand.

"Songs and Seniors" was founded to bridge the gap between an ideal world with individualized music therapy sessions for all, and the financial realities of long-term care. Comprised mostly of group sessions, "Songs and Seniors" offers two different types of groups, Music Therapy Groups and Music Activity Groups, to both meet the needs of Austin-area seniors, and to provide flexible and financially sustainable options for long-term care centers. Music Therapy Groups are closed groups, limited to only six to eight regular participants, and are structured around a formalized treatment plan with

clearly defined goals and objectives. Each participant's individual progress is documented at every session. Groups are designed to build and maintain functional goals in areas such as cognition and memory, fine and gross motor skills, social skills and increased socialization, and emotional support and expression. Music Activity Groups are broader in scope and application and contain no written treatment plan, but are still grounded in all of the same music therapy principles and techniques. Music Activity Groups are open to a greater number of participants and designed to be engaging and beneficial for seniors across a wider range of functional abilities. Music Activity Groups are a budget-friendly way of introducing the benefits of music therapy to a community as well. Most importantly, the "Songs and Seniors" program has allowed me to bring music therapy into communities across the greater Austin area, many of which have never had music therapy as a part of their program before, and to share the joy of music with a too often forgotten generation.

In this book I have compiled some of my favorite ideas and session plans created and developed within the "Songs and Seniors" program. While this book is in no way a comprehensive guide to working with seniors as a music therapist, it is exactly the sort of book I am always on the lookout for: a book of ideas. It is meant to be short and sweet, simple, and most of all, easy to use. Many great authors have written extensively on the research behind music therapy with the senior population or on the theories and principles involved in the practice of music therapy with geriatrics. This is not that book. This book is meant for music therapists, from students to veterans of the field, who are simply looking for new ideas to engage seniors in joyful music therapy sessions.

I have loved creating a program that is 100% musically driven and that offers something for every senior, at all areas of needs and abilities. This program is full of sessions that always seek to incorporate a variety of instruments and musical offerings for seniors to enjoy. Sessions are designed to both challenge seniors with new ideas and approaches to music making, and to delight them with familiar and much-loved musical favorites. I am thrilled to share this series of sessions as I enjoy leading them, as much as my seniors enjoy participating in them, and I am excited for you and your seniors to enjoy them too.

THE UPS AND DOWNS OF WORKING WITH SENIORS

Most of my peers couldn't understand or relate when I discussed my dream of working with seniors and hospice towards the end of my high school years. A few family members questioned, "Isn't that going to be kind of depressing? Wouldn't you rather work with children who can actually *get better*?" And it's true; ultimately seniors are at the latter part of their lives, their health is in general or serious decline, and there is nothing anyone can do to stop it. But I felt passionately then and I feel passionately now that seniors still deserve the chance to engage in life as fully as possible, to work to maintain and improve their health as much as possible, and to continue to grow and learn new skills. As with any other population, there are ups and downs to choosing a career in working with seniors, from dealing with the inevitable situations that approaching the end of life brings, to more practical issues of budget and health care costs. I of course believe the rewards far outweigh the challenges, and if you are reading this book, most likely you do too. However, taking an honest look at the ups and downs of practicing music therapy with the senior population will only make you a better therapist and a better advocate.

Seniors themselves are a unique population. There are huge variations in abilities, needs, and personalities amongst seniors as everyone ages differently and each senior's current situation is the culmination of decades of different experiences and challenges. A vast array of life events and personalities, which have developed over many years, create a blend of strengths, difficulties, and perspectives unique to each senior. Though some seniors may have experienced serious health declines and need significant assistance and support, they are still adults and need to be treated as such. The challenge then as a therapist becomes providing the assistance they need and creating interventions that reach them at their current level of functioning, while still respecting them as adults. Many seniors may be sensitive to interventions that appear "childish," or attempts to assist them that come off as "treating them like children" while other seniors may love that exact same song or intervention and respond enthusiastically. As a therapist, I find it often comes down to presentation. As long as I am speaking and presenting a particular intervention in a way that addresses them in a mature manner, they enjoy participating without reservations. Some seniors may choose not to participate or may not want to work in a music therapy session, and sometimes, quite frankly, they would rather sleep. As a therapist, you need know when to push them and when to respect that they are adults who have every right to make that choice. Working with seniors means needing to be comfortable with end of life issues and with the fact that you are working with a patient who is ultimately not going to recover. When working with children, there is almost always a focus of working with hope towards a long future. With seniors, it is much more about the here and now and helping them to get the most out of their lives today.

One of the biggest challenges in choosing to focus on working with seniors is a lack of funding. This is regardless of whether you are an employee at a single facility or a contractor working at multiple communities. I will speak mostly from a contractor's perspective. However, it should be duly noted that even full time employees are not immune from budget issues and dealing with concerns such as low pay, work overload, and an insufficient budget for support staff and supplies. I work in many long-term care communities and all of them are constantly dealing with tight budgets and frequent budget cuts. As health care costs continue to soar and people continue to live longer, the reality is that the costs of already expensive long-term care will only continue to increase. Additionally, though it may sound callous, as a society we are more focused on the younger generations. People are willing to stretch their budgets and do what it takes to provide services for their children, but are much less likely to do so for aging parents. The challenge for music therapists is to provide quality services, which prove the value of music therapy, while maintaining rates that are indicative of the level of training MT-BCs have completed, while still offering cost-effective options. However, while you may have to work extra hard to create that room in the budget for music therapy, the senior population is growing, meaning the market for music therapy services with

seniors is also expanding. No doubt, budgets will remain tight, but census (the number of seniors living in a particular facility), is closely tied to that community's budget. Therefore, if a music therapy program gives a facility a competitive edge in the marketplace, thereby increasing their census, there will be room in that budget for music therapy services.

While budget and rising long-term care costs can make it difficult to start a music therapy program for seniors, staff turnover presents an additional challenge. Many communities I marketed to and worked with went through three activity coordinators (my first contact at many places) and two executive directors in a two-year period. Initially, I found staff turnover to be extremely frustrating, as after working so hard to start a program at a particular community, I would find myself starting all over with explaining the value of music therapy to someone new. Plus I knew there was always the threat that the new hire or new management company would see my rate and cut my program almost immediately. However, the longer I am in the profession, I find that staff turnover is much less of a problem. First of all, many of the "best" communities to work at (those that are the easiest to work with and contracting the greatest number of music therapy hours) have the least amount of staff turnover and the greatest overall stability. When I do lose a group to frequent staff turnover, it suggests that I was less likely to be successful in retaining them as a long-term client and/or increasing their number of music therapy hours anyway. While staff members may leave one facility, I've learned that those most passionate about quality services for seniors are not leaving the field of senior care and I often end up with a familiar contact at a new community. Over the years, many times an individual did not hire me at first, but later went on to hire me after he or she had changed jobs to a different facility with a higher budget. Also remember, while initially high staff turnover may feel incredibly discouraging, ultimately, every connection you make further establishes your presence in the field of senior care, which could very well lead to a contract down the road. Furthermore, those facilities with the highest staff turnover have the highest staff turnover for a reason and they probably would not become the long-term clients you want, no matter how well you do your job.

Another challenge in providing music therapy services to seniors is the huge variation of abilities within a single group, even in small groups. Group music therapy sessions are a popular choice with the senior population because increasing socialization and decreasing isolation are major goal areas for seniors and of course are best achieved in a group session. Groups are also a more budget friendly option. While in an ideal world, everyone would be placed in a group based on their needs and abilities, that is often not the case due to the general lack of funding, especially in today's market. This means that there is a very good chance you will be asked to lead groups comprised both of seniors who are socially and cognitively high functioning and those who are almost or completely non-responsive. It can be very frustrating to see both sets of seniors not getting what could benefit them the most because they are combined in the same group. It is also difficult in that scenario to plan sessions that offer everyone as much as possible. The reality of the situation is, when a nursing home can only afford a very limited number of dollars for group music therapy services, they want as many residents to participate as possible. This restricts individual residents from benefitting fully. I recognize this is not an ideal situation for anyone. Instead of becoming frustrated by this reality, understand that while many facilities cannot afford the ideal level of service, they are still working to provide as much benefit to their residents as they can. While I could choose not to lead those groups, doing so would most likely mean **no** music therapy services at all for those seniors. Practically speaking, given the realities

of the current market, it would put a dent in my business as well. At the end of the day, I would rather ALL of those seniors be able to participate in musical interventions designed to support them and help them to improve and maintain their functional abilities and quality of life as much as possible, even in a less than ideal situation. It can be difficult to structure a group around varied needs and abilities, but the huge advantage of music in this setting is its adaptability. In a collaborative musical experience, non-verbal seniors can play an instrument or move along with the music while verbal seniors can sing. Those with higher cognitive functioning can be assigned more difficult parts, such as playing a hand bell on cue, while those with more challenges can be given a simpler part, such as shaking a maraca along with the entire song. The possibilities are endless. Your ability to involve seniors across a wide range of functional skills in a single group session can also be one of the strongest selling points of a music therapy program. While sometimes groups based on similar needs and abilities may be the most beneficial therapeutically, I have come to appreciate the advantages of mixed-ability groups as well (within reasonable limits). The increased energy and enthusiastic participation of some tends to pull others with more challenges to a higher level of participation.

Given all the challenges of working with the senior population, it is vital to not lose sight of all the wonderful things that come with a career spent practicing music therapy with the elderly. First of all, seniors love music. They are from a generation that grew up without iPods and CD players. In their generation, enjoyment of music was inherently social, and without ready access to an endless offering of recorded music, music required active participation. Many seniors still love actively engaging in music, generating group music therapy sessions that truly are a lot of fun. Retirement offers a time of life with little pressure, with extra time to enjoy life and develop new skills and hobbies. Seniors still want, need, and love the opportunity to try new things, and oftentimes they still want to grow and develop new skills. Many seniors feel less restrained by social convention and are free to try new things without the fear of failure. Furthermore, seniors have a lifetime of experiences and wisdom to draw upon, which makes working with them a rich and rewarding experience.

On a more personal note, I am passionate about working with seniors as I do not want to see them becoming isolated in facilities, disconnected from the rest of the community and without access to the richness music can bring to life. I truly believe we lose something as a society when we stop looking towards the wisdom and experiences of an older generation. We lose perspective when we only focus on the here and now of today and can't take the time to see life through someone who has already lived through a lot more of it than us. And of course, you will never find more positive, funny, and encouraging individuals than you will meet through music therapy sessions with seniors.

As with any other population, there are both upsides and downsides to a career in music therapy with seniors. While it can be difficult at times, none of the challenges are insurmountable and the joy and the rewards that come with it are great.

WHAT'S IN YOUR STASH?

I truly believe an ample supply of quality instruments is necessary for the success of any music therapy program, especially when working with seniors. I never cease to be amazed by how **much** seniors love trying and playing a variety of instruments. Even those who are initially reluctant to participate otherwise, will often try a drum, maraca, bell, or whatever else is presented. Also, anyone can lead a sing-along (and many non-music therapists do just that). Your ability to incorporate a wealth of musical offerings and experiences is part of what sets you apart as a therapist and makes you more marketable in today's world of senior care. Whether you are developing a music therapy program for seniors as part or all of your own business, or creating or maintaining a music therapy program within a single facility, budget and funding will most likely be a limiting factor. Of course your preferences and music therapy style will influence what types of instruments you choose to buy. The types of instruments you buy will in turn influence the type of sessions and interventions you lead. If you find yourself in a rut, I would encourage you to break out of your comfort zone and utilize instruments that may not be the ones you reach for first. Try something new. It will help expand your creative horizons as a therapist and your seniors will probably love it!

Ultimately, how you decide to build your stash of musical fun is totally up to you. If you are just starting out, knowing what instruments will be the best fit for your program as well as knowing how to get the most for the money you **do** have to spend can be daunting. This section is here to provide some guidance. Keep in mind that the instruments you place in your seniors' hands will be driving your program so this is NOT an area in which to scrimp and save. A quality and varied collection of functional and fun instruments will be the best thing you can do for your senior music therapy program. Remember, seniors are adults; therefore authentic instruments (rather than children's versions) are best.

I've broken down my recommendations for building an instrument collection for a vibrant, senior music therapy program into three lists—Bare Basics, Fill Out Your Collection, Nice Additions—to help you prioritize your budget. Of course there are a myriad of other possibilities, but this is a good overview of a functional, fun, and varied collection. Quantities will depend on your unique situation. This particular list is based on groups that range in size from six to 30 people in a variety of settings.

I am assuming that you, as the therapist, will be leading on guitar. Whatever guitar you choose to use really comes down to personal preference, so I will not make any guitar recommendations, except to suggest you own at least two. If guitar is your lead instrument, you do not want to be struggling to lead sessions when your guitar breaks.

 Instrument Collection Recommendations

Bare Basics

- 10 Paddle Drums and/or Nesting Hand Drums
- 10 Mallets
- 1 20-Note Chromatic Hand Bell Set
- 3 Tambourines
- 12 Maracas
- 12 Jingle Bells (cluster or rhythm and wrist)
- 12-36 LP Brand Conga Shakers (or Egg Shakers)

Fill Out Your Collection

- 4 Eight-Note Boomwhacker Sets
- Ocean Drum
- 3-4 Large Cabasas
- 3-4 Small Cabasas
- Additional Drums and Tambourines
- Additional Maracas, Bells, and Shakers as desired

Nice Additions

- 12-36 Slide Whistles
- Xylophone (more useful with smaller groups)
- Various other small percussion instruments such as:
  - ~ Cymbals
  - ~ Triangle
  - ~ Wood Blocks
  - ~ Wooden Clapper
  - ~ Clatterpiller
  - ~ Monk Bell
  - ~ Agogo Bells
  - ~ Rasping Frog
  - ~ Washboard
  - ~ Rainstick
- Small, Ethnic Instruments from around the World (ex. Seed Shakers)
- Kazoos*

I purchase relatively cheap kazoos in bulk and allow seniors to keep them after we use them in a session. They are really not built to last and are too difficult to sanitize properly.

 Some Special Considerations and Brand Recommendations

Drums: Some therapists I know prefer nesting hand drums, as they are more compact and easier to transport. I find paddle drums are much easier for many of my seniors to use. Both drums have a great, authentic drum sound. I actually have both in my "stash" as some seniors are more successful with paddle drums, while others have the full use of only one hand and hand drums can easily rest on their wheelchair tray or a nearby table. Having a variety of sizes can be fun (and frequently it's more cost effective to buy drums in sets that contain a variety of sizes) but do note that the larger paddle drums available will often prove too heavy for many seniors to handle and use effectively.

Maracas: There are a lot of maracas on the market, many of which are wooden and beautifully painted. While I own a few of the traditional red and green wooden maracas, the bulk of my collection is made up of Toca brand black plastic maracas in large and small sizes. Though less visually appealing, the sound quality is very good and they are louder than other versions. Too many times one of my seniors has chosen one of the wooden maracas only to shake it and say, "This one doesn't do anything," because he or she cannot hear it. Toca maracas are also extremely durable and easy to clean. That being said, I still include some wooden, more visually appealing maracas, as well, to provide choices, and some seniors prefer a more aesthetically pleasing appearance above sound quality.

Egg Shakers/Conga Shakers: While egg shakers are a popular choice for many music therapists in a variety of settings, I gravitate more towards the LP brand Conga Shakers in some group settings, again due to volume concerns as the conga shakers are louder than the egg shakers. I purchased a big box containing a variety of colors when I first started the program and they have worked well for years.

Cabasas: Though I personally much prefer the feel of the larger wooden cabasas, I would suggest including both some of the larger wooden ones and the smaller plastic cabasas in your collection. The wooden cabasas are heavier and some seniors have a much easier time using the lighter version.

Jingle Bells: Most of my jingle bells are the (3 bell) cluster bells or the (5 bell) rhythm bells. However, I never go to a group without a few of the wrist bell sets with Velcro for those seniors who are unable to grasp any sort of instrument. Every time I pull out those wrist bells to use with seniors with physical challenges, their faces light up as soon as they realize they can still play along!

HOW TO MAKE THE MOST OF THIS BOOK

This book is designed to be more of a reference manual for music therapists, rather than an in-depth discussion of music therapy with the senior population. Every music therapist has his or her own unique style, approach, and ideas, but if you're like me, you are probably always in search of other creative approaches and new ideas to incorporate into your music therapy sessions. Perhaps a new way to engage your clients in music, something that will excite them or motivate them, or maybe a more effective or a more fun way of promoting skill development and skill maintenance. The rest of this book is a collection of session outlines, ideas, and resources.

All of the session outlines, ideas, and additional resources contained in this book have been tested and utilized in numerous music therapy groups. In fact, **ALL** of the session plans contained in this book have been successfully implemented in independent living communities, assisted living communities, skilled nursing units, memory care units, and day programs. While not every intervention in every plan will be effective with all senior groups, each plan as a whole contains enough adaptable materials, which with some modification, can be used to effectively meet a wide range of needs, abilities, and goals.

The next part of this book contains a series of session plans all designed around a central, topical theme and are for groups that last approximately an hour. Each session plan contains a one-page outline of the session and a page of additional resources designed to make leading that session a bit easier. For each of my sessions, I like to have all the information I need right at my finger tips. This way I do not have to try to remember specific group discussion questions or fact-check my recollection of things such as the history of Memorial Day and how best to present it in a clear and concise manner. As discussed earlier, each of these sessions have been used in a variety of group settings with seniors with a variety of needs and abilities. **This means that every intervention described has been tested and tweaked to ensure it is both effective and enjoyable.** I tried to document each outline so that it is as close as possible to how I have used that session plan with a group. That being said, none of these session outlines are written in stone and you should feel free to modify and adapt ideas and song choices to best meet the needs of your seniors. I never present the same session in exactly the same way as there are huge variations in needs and abilities between my groups, and even variations within a given group from week to week as well. As therapists we are trained to adapt and adjust to the needs of the moment and the changing needs of the group. Of course many changes also need to be made when presenting similar material to seniors in independent living communities and in memory care units. Occasionally, modifications are recorded in the session outlines, but mostly I trust you as a music therapist to be able to make the necessary skill-level adjustments to meet the specific needs of your seniors.

The format of each outline is designed to be as consistent as possible to ensure ease of use. All songs and musical selections utilized in the session are in bold font to make it easy to see at a glance all the songs involved in that particular plan. Unless specified as "recorded" or otherwise, all songs are sung live as a group with the therapist leading on guitar. Many sessions contain theme-related songs that are familiar to seniors, although additional help is most likely needed with the lyrics. These songs are included in song packets. Song packets are nothing more than a stapled collection of lyrics (one page per song) with page numbers and a cover with the name of the theme for easy reference. I make a copy for myself as well with the chords I prefer to use included for songs I do not know by heart. Song Packets are passed out to each participant during the session immediately prior to singing the songs included in them, and collected afterwards to avoid distraction when we are working with instruments or on another intervention. Please note that song lyrics are protected under copyright law and use careful consideration when using printed versions of lyrics. Many of the songs suggested in this book are not considered in the public domain so please be sure your use of all copyrighted materials falls under the guidelines of fair use. This is another good reason to collect song packets immediately after they are used in the session. "Shakeables" is another intervention that appears with some regularity. "Shakeables" is my own special designation for a collection of instruments that can be played by shaking such

as maracas, cluster bells, tambourines, shakers, etc. Whenever I lead an intervention that calls for shaking along on an instrument, I like to bring a variety so seniors can have a choice and also have the chance to try new things from session to session. "Shakeables" is an easy way to describe this. My "shakeables" collection for any given group typically includes one dozen shakers, one dozen cluster bells/wrist bells, one dozen maracas, three tambourines, and a few less familiar instruments such as seed shakers, shekeres, etc.

Also note that session outlines may reference things available in Part Three: Additional Resources. Many of the sessions start with singing "popular/favorite" songs. Most of the time I like to warm up my groups with songs they all know by heart. A list of the songs well known and loved by my seniors can be found in Part Three. Also several session outlines contain a drum circle as a part of the session plan. Tips and ideas for leading a simple but fun drum circle with your seniors can also be found in Part Three. Movement ideas for movement to music exercises and a variety of shaking patterns for those "shakeables" are available in Part Three as well.

Part Three of this book contains an assortment of additional resources, some designed to compliment the material of Part Two and some to serve as a quick reference guide to song/musical suggestions and additional ideas to incorporate into your senior music therapy program. Included are several song lists and favorite recorded music mixes for easy reference. Ideas for using a variety of instruments and drumming are included as well. Please note that drumming, while immensely popular with my seniors, is only lightly touched upon, as there are already numerous resources available that deal exclusively with drumming as a treatment modality. However, I did want to include some of the ways I introduce and start to incorporate drumming with my senior groups.

Theme-Based Session Plans

PART TWO

OUTLINE: *Introductory Session*

NOTE: *For my program, I use this session as my free sample session. I think it makes a great first session for any senior group as it presents a low-key introduction to trying different instruments and allows a therapist to get to know everyone a little bit. It also offers activities at varying ability levels, which is important as you never know what kind of response you are going to get when you walk into a facility for the first time.*

Opening:

Lead seniors in singing along with several popular/favorite songs. Include a few slower songs and plenty of upbeat songs.

Movement to Music:

Have the group sing-along and move as you play and sing, **"When the Saints Go Marching In."** Add a different movement direction to move with the beat every two verses.

Shakeable Instruments:

Introduce the maracas, jingle bells, tambourines, and shakers. Pass out instruments to each group member, offering them at least two different choices. Encourage everyone to at least try an instrument. For example, if someone initially rejects playing an instrument, I ask them to just shake it 3x and if they don't like it, they can hand it right back. They will almost always decide they want to play along. Have seniors shake along while singing the song, **"Jingle Jangle Jingle."**

Instrumental Performance:

Have everyone hold onto their instruments to shake along with the song, **"Rock Around the Clock."** After the last written verse, modify the song to include directions as to how to play the instruments such as: "We're going to shake up high, shake up high, shake, shake to the sky...". Include directions to play high, low, to the side, fast, slow, loud, and soft.

Group Songwriting:

Rewrite the song, **"My Favorite Things,"** as a group, singing instead about all of the group's favorite things, including favorite activities, hobbies, foods, etc. Try to get at least one response from each group member with as much prompting as needed. Once the song is finished, sing it together 2x.

Drumming:

Introduce the paddle drums and/or hand drums and demonstrate how to play them. Ask for volunteers to try a drum and prompt individuals as needed. Oftentimes seniors need a little extra encouragement to try something new, especially if this is their first session. Lead everyone to play together on a steady beat. Keep this steady beat going as the group sings, **"I've Been Working on the Railroad."** Then change the drum pattern to a long-short-long (think dotted quarter note, eighth note, dotted quarter etc.) and have seniors drum the new pattern while singing the song again.

Closing:

Lead the group in singing the song, **"Farewell Ladies, Farewell Gentlemen."**

ADDITIONAL RESOURCES:

"When the Saints Go Marching In" Movement to Music

"Oh, When the saints go marching in..." etc. **Tap Toes**

"Oh, When the sun begins to shine..." etc. **Tap Toes**

"Oh, When the saints go marching in..." etc. **March In Place**

"Oh, When the choir begins to sing...." etc. **March in Place**

"Oh, When the saints go marching in..." etc. **Pat Knees**

"Oh, When the preacher begins to preach..." etc. **Pat Knees**

"Oh, When the saints go marching in..." etc. **Clap Hands**

"Oh, When the trumpet begins to sound..." etc. **Clap Hands**

"Oh, When the saints go marching in..." etc.(2x) **Clap and March in Place**

"Our Favorite Things" Songwriting

To the (recommended) tune of "My Favorite Things"

_____and_____

_____and_____

_____and_____and_____and_____

These are a few of our favorite things!

_____and_____

_____and_____

_____and_____and_____and_____

These are a few of our favorite things!

When_____, When_____

When we're feeling sad-

We simply remember our favorite things,

And then we don't feel so bad!

OUTLINE: *Sun, Moon, & Stars*

Opening/Introduce Theme:

Lead seniors in singing along with several popular/favorite songs. Include a few slower songs and plenty of upbeat songs. Then introduce the theme of songs about the Sun, Moon, and Stars.

Fill-In-The-Blank Song Titles:

Have seniors complete a fill-in-the blank style activity, verbally completing song titles as a group that are about the sun, the moon, or the stars. Say the first word or phrase of a song title and see if they can complete that title.

Movement to Music:

Lead a movement to music exercise with a recording of the song, "Old Devil Moon," by Frank Sinatra. Give a variety of movement directions throughout the song. See Part Three for ideas.

Song Packets and Related Exercises:

Pass out song packets containing lyrics to all of the following songs to each group participant. Sing each song as a group and complete related exercises as indicated. See resources as needed.

- "Fly Me to the Moon"
- "By the Light of the Silvery Moon"
- "On Moonlight Bay"– Sing through 2x, then add hand bells, forming chords, to accompany.
- "Moon River"
- "Blue Moon"
- "When You Wish Upon a Star"

Group Discussion:

After singing, "When You Wish Upon A Star," discuss wishes on stars as a group. Discussion prompts could include: "What stars do you make wishes on?" (shooting stars, falling stars, first star in the evening, etc.) "Have you ever wished on a star?" "What did you wish for?" "Did it come true?" "If you saw the first star tonight, what *would* you wish for?"

Shakeable Instruments:

Pass out small percussion instruments and shake along as a group while singing two songs, "Shine on, Harvest Moon" and "You Are My Sunshine."

Drumming:

Lead seniors in drumming along with a recording of the march, "Stars and Stripes Forever," giving them cues to play loud, soft, on the drumhead, on the rim, etc.

Closing:

Pass out additional drums and percussion instruments as needed and lead seniors in a drum circle.

ADDITIONAL RESOURCES:

Sun, Moon, & Stars Song Titles

"Blue Moon"

"Fly Me to the Moon"

"Old Devil Moon"

"When You Wish Upon a Star"

"Twinkle, Twinkle, Little Star"

"You Are My Sunshine"

"Moon River"

"By the Light of the Silvery Moon"

"Shine On, Harvest Moon"

"On Moonlight Bay"

"It's Only a Paper Moon"

"How High the Moon"

"Stars and Stripes Forever"

"Stardust"

"Catch a Falling Star"

"Here Comes the Sun"

 Introducing and Using the Hand Bells

NOTE: *This is often the session I use when introducing the hand bells for the first time.*

Before doing a song with a hand bell accompaniment, I like to give seniors a brief demonstration and explanation of how the hand bells work. Even if we have done hand bells before, some group members may have forgotten or some group members may be new.

I start by demonstrating that all one needs to do to play a hand bell is to hold it firmly by the handle and give it a shake. I explain and demonstrate that each hand bell is a different color as each bell has its own unique pitch, and that when played together they can create harmony. I then pass out the bells, (asking for volunteers) dividing the group into sections by chords, so that seniors who need to play together are also seated in the same area. I usually start with just one chord at a time and ask everyone playing that chord to

practice starting and stopping together on my cue a few times. I remind the group to play when I am facing them and gesturing to them, but to stop when I turn away so each section gets a "solo." Working together this way we are able to create an accompaniment. First, I practice with each chord section alone, then I practice with all the sections, switching between chords until everyone is fairly comfortable with starting and stopping and following my cues. Then we try the entire song together with everyone singing along while using the hand bells to provide the accompaniment.

"On Moonlight Bay" only requires three different chords: D, A, and G, and is generally a fairly easy accompaniment pattern to follow on the hand bells!

OUTLINE: *New Year's*

Opening/Introduce Theme:

Lead seniors in singing along with several popular/favorite songs. Include a few slower songs and plenty of upbeat songs. Then introduce the theme of celebrating the New Year.

Movement to Music:

Lead a movement to music exercise with a recording of the song, **"Ringin' in a Brand New Year."** Give a variety of movement directions throughout the song. See Part Three for ideas.

Song Packets and Related Exercises:

Pass out song packets containing lyrics to all of the following songs to each group participant. Sing each song as a group and complete related exercises as indicated. See resources as needed.

- *"Auld Lang Syne"*– First introduce the song and discuss the meaning of the lyrics, then sing.

Ask seniors to list and discuss various ways to celebrate the New Year. Use the discussion to lead into the next song.

- **"I Could Have Danced All Night"**
- **"Sentimental Journey"**– Before singing this song, discuss the New Year as a time not just to look ahead, but also to reflect upon and take a "sentimental journey" through the previous year. Ask seniors to share favorite memories and events from the previous year.
- *"Que Sera, Sera"*– Discuss how we don't know what the New Year will bring. Ask seniors if taking a "whatever will be, will be" approach is good advice.

Ask seniors if anyone made resolutions for the New Year and make a list as a group. Use the next two songs to suggest some positive resolutions seniors could adopt.

- **"Accentuate the Positive"**– Resolve to be more positive and focus on the good things in life!
- **"Getting to Know You"**– Resolve to make a new friend or two within the community. Discuss ways seniors can meet new people or get to know someone new.
- *"Vive La Compagnie"*– Remind seniors that no matter what the New Year brings, we will always have friends by our side!

Group Songwriting and Hand Bells:

Have the group complete a fill-in-the-blank style song writing exercise about hopes for the New Year. One recommendation is to the tune of the song, **"It's a Small World."** After the song is completed, add hand bells to create the accompaniment. Use hand bells to create the chords, D, A, and G. See additional resources for the session, "Sun, Moon, & Stars" for ideas on effectively leading a chordal accompaniment with the hand bells.

Closing:

Lead seniors in a movement to music exercise with a recording of the song, **"Let's Start the New Year Right."** Give a variety of movement directions throughout the song. See Part Three for ideas.

ADDITIONAL RESOURCES:

Meaning of "Auld Lang Syne"

Ask seniors if anyone knows what *auld lang syne* means. Explain how while the literal translation is "old long since," it can be more loosely translated as, "for the sake of long ago," or "for the sake of old times." Essentially the song is saying to remember times gone by and most specifically to remember long lasting friendships. It is sung at New Year's to remind us to remember the past, and to call to mind those nearest and dearest to us.

Examples of Ways to Celebrate the New Year

- Parties with friends
- Drinking
- Champagne toast (and a kiss!) at midnight
- Dancing
- Making resolutions
- Fireworks/firecrackers
- Noisemakers
- New Year's Day Rose Parade/ Rose Bowl
- Watching the ball drop in New York City on television
- Family Traditions

New Year's Songwriting

To the (recommended) tune of "It's a Small World"

We want a year of _____

And a year of _____

We hope for _____ and _____

And a year of _____

It's with joy that we sing

Hopes a New Year will bring

It's a New Year after all!

Chorus:

It's a New Year after all,

It's a New Year after all,

It's a New Year after all,

It's a New Year after all!

OUTLINE: *1920s*

Opening:

Lead seniors in singing along with three popular songs from the 1920s: **"Five Foot Two, Eyes of Blue," "Side by Side,"** and **"Yes Sir, That's My Baby."** Share the story behind the song, "Yes Sir, That's My Baby."

Introduce Theme:

Briefly introduce the theme of the 1920s. The 1920s were known as the "Roaring Twenties" and also as the "Jazz Age." Jazz music gained popularity during this time and speakeasies, clubs that served illegal liquor, (also known as "bootleg hooch"), came into being. Al Capone, a notorious gangster, made his fortune selling bootleg beer. Discuss how Prohibition started in 1919 and didn't end until the 1930s, etc.

Movement to Music:

Lead a movement to music exercise with a recording of two songs, **"Swanee"** and **"Sweet Georgia Brown."** Give a variety of movement directions throughout the songs. See Part Three for ideas.

Group Discussion:

Read different slang phrases that originated during the 1920s. Ask seniors what each phrase means and discuss. Many of these phrases are still used today!

Shakeable Instruments:

Pass out a variety of instruments and shake along with the following recorded songs.

- **"Charleston"** by Paul Whiteman – Direct seniors to shake along in various ways with the rhythm of this piece. See Part Three for ideas.
- **"Pinetop's Boogie Woogie"** by Pinetop Smith – Pinetop Smith gives directions to start and stop moving during this song. Have seniors start and stop shaking, following the directions he gives.

Song Packets and Related Exercises:

Pass out song packets containing lyrics to all of the following songs to each group participant. Sing each song as a group and complete related exercises as indicated. See resources as needed.

- **"Ain't We Got Fun"**– After singing it through once, instruct seniors to emphasize the word "fun," shouting it each time it appears in the song. Then sing it through again with the added vocal emphasis.
- **"Bye, Bye, Blackbird"**
- **"Carolina in the Morning"**
- **"My Blue Heaven"**– Possibly have seniors add an accompaniment on the ocean drum and/or the rain stick to accentuate the peaceful flow of this popular song.
- **"Tiptoe Through the Tulips"**
- **"I Wanna Be Loved By You"**
- **"Yes! We Have No Bananas"**

Event Timeline:

Have seniors take turns drawing from an array of cards, each with a picture and/or description of an event of the 1920s to share with the group before placing the card in the appropriate place on a 1920s timeline.

Closing:

Lead a movement to music exercise with a recording of the song, **"Toot, Toot, Tootsie! Goodbye."** Give a variety of movement directions throughout the song. See Part Three for ideas.

ADDITIONAL RESOURCES:

Fun Song Facts

"Yes Sir! That's My Baby" was actually inspired by a mechanical pig. According to one story, the songwriters, Donaldson and Kahn, were visiting Eddie Cantor. His daughter, Marjorie, brought out a mechanical pig, one of her favorite toys. It started walking in rhythm while playing two notes, which inspired the basis for the song.

"Pinetop's Boogie Woogie" is an important song as Pinetop Smith was a major influence on the "boogie woogie" style. His song was later arranged and recorded by Tommy Dorsey and his orchestra in 1938, eventually becoming Dorsey's best selling record with over 5 million copies sold. It was incredibly popular both during and after World War II.

1920s Slang

All Wet: An incorrect or inaccurate idea or individual

Baloney: Nonsense

Bee's Knees: Terrific; a fantastic person, thing, or idea

Beef: A complaint

Beeswax: Business, as in "None of your beeswax"

Big Cheese: An important person, the boss

Blind Date: A date with someone you do not know

Cat's Meow: Something that's great, the best

Crush: An infatuation

Dogs: Feet

Doll: An attractive woman

Dolled Up: All dressed up

Dough: Money

Flat Tire: A boring individual or a disappointing date

Frame: To set someone up, giving false evidence

Gams: A woman's legs

Giggle Water: Alcohol, booze

Hard-boiled: Tough, as in a tough guy

Hike: A walk, as in "Take a hike!"

Hoof: To walk

Keen: Appealing, attractive

Knee Duster: Skirt

Jalopy: An old car

Line: A false story, as in "to feed one a line"

Nifty: Great, excellent

Ossified: Drunk

Pinch: To arrest. Pinched: to be arrested

Pushover: A person easily convinced

Real McCoy: A genuine item or person

Ritzy: Elegant

Scram: To leave immediately

Spiffy: Looking good

Upchuck: To vomit

What's eating you?: What's wrong?

Events of the 1920s

1920 The 19th Amendment gives women the right to vote

1920 The first assembly of the League of Nations is held

1921 Babe Ruth sets record of 137 career home runs

1922 Creation of the USSR (Union of Soviet Socialist Republics)

1923 *Time Magazine* publishes its first issue

1924 The first winter Olympic Games are held in France

1925 "Balto" the dog is a hero after hauling much-needed diphtheria medication by dogsled in Alaska

1925 "Monkey Trial" ends and John Scopes is found guilty of teaching Darwinism in school

1926 NBC Radio Network opens with 24 stations

1927 Charles Lindbergh makes the first solo, non-stop, transatlantic flight from New York to Paris

1927 The world population reaches 2 billion people

1928 The first US air-conditioned office building opens in San Antonio, TX

1928 Scotch Tape is invented by the 3M Company

1929 "Popeye" makes his first appearance

1929 The stock market crashes, starting the Great Depression

OUTLINE: *Country & Western*

Opening:

Pass out drums and a variety of percussion instruments and lead seniors in a drum circle.

Introduce Theme/Maracas and Bells:

Introduce today's theme of "country & western music."

Sing the song, **"Jingle Jangle Jingle,"** with instruments. Divide the group into two sections and pass out maracas to one section and bells to the other. Direct the seniors with maracas to play during the verses and the seniors with the bells to play during the chorus. Sing the song through as a group with the maracas and bells adding to the accompaniment at the appropriate times.

Movement to Music:

Lead the group in a choreographed movement to music exercise with a recording of the song, **"Sixteen Tons."** Teach seniors the sequence of movements first, then perform it all together as a group with the music.

Song Packets and Related Exercises:

Pass out song packets containing lyrics to all of the following songs to each group participant. Sing each song as a group and complete related exercises as indicated. See resources as needed.

- **"Hey, Good Lookin'"**
- **"San Antonio Rose"**
- **"The Tennessee Waltz"**– Add maracas and drums to accompany.
- **"Home on the Range"**
- **"The Yellow Rose of Texas"**
- **"Take Me Home, Country Roads"**

Movement to Music:

Lead the group in modified country line dancing to a recording of the song, **"Why Baby Why?"**

Have seniors hold hands to form a line as they complete the movements.

Closing:

Lead the group in singing the song, **"Happy Trails,"** 2x.

ADDITIONAL RESOURCES:

"Sixteen Tons" Choreographed Dance

Progressive Movement Sequence
All movements performed while seated.

Verse One ~ Clap Hands
Chorus and Verse Two ~ Clap Hands and Tap Toes
Chorus and Verse Three ~ Tap Toes and Pat Knees
Chorus and Verse Four ~ Tap Toes while alternating between
Clapping Hands and Patting Knees
Final Chorus ~ Clap Hands and March

"The Tennessee Waltz" with Maracas and Bells

Since this song is a familiar one for most seniors, I like to add drums and maracas in an accompaniment pattern for this session. Following the waltz pattern, the drums play on the downbeat 1, while the maracas play on the off beats 2 and 3. Most seniors catch on fairly quickly, though it helps to practice the instruments alone, first while counting, then as the therapist sings a verse, before the entire group sings the song with the added instrumental parts. For lower functioning groups, I like to have seniors put the waltz in their bodies, swaying (while seated) side to side with the beat.

Modified Country Line Dancing to "Why Baby Why"

I make a big deal out of the fact that we are doing "country line dancing" as opposed to just moving with the music as it encourages seniors to enthusiastically get into the spirit of the activity. I have them start by holding hands to form a line and then practice all of the movements first, before we perform it with the music. Also, once the movements have been taught, this can be used as a memory exercise by performing the song 2x. On the second time through, ask seniors to recall all of the movements with no additional prompts.

1) Tap toes during opening/first chorus

2) Kick alternating feet, starting right foot first during the first verse

3) Tap toes during the chorus

4) Rock side to side during the instrumental interlude

5) Move alternating shoulders up and down starting with the right shoulder first, during the next verse

6) Tap toes during the final chorus

OUTLINE: *Love*

Opening:

Pass out small percussion instruments and lead seniors in singing and shaking along with several upbeat popular/favorite songs.

Introduce Theme/Reminiscence/ Group Discussion:

Introduce today's theme of "Love" and discuss Valentine's Day, if seasonally appropriate. Ask seniors to think about their sweethearts—maybe a sweetheart from a long time ago who still holds a special place in their heart, maybe a sweetheart they have been married to for many, many years, or maybe a special someone they have just recently gotten to know. Encourage them to think about their special someone as they sing, **"Let Me Call You Sweetheart"** as a group 2x. Possibly have the group all hold hands and sway side to side with the rhythm of the song as they sing. After singing, ask each senior to tell the group about his or her sweetheart.

Movement to Music:

Lead a movement to music exercise with a recording of the song, **"Love and Marriage,"** by Frank Sinatra. Give a variety of movement directions throughout the song. See Part Three for ideas.

Singing in a Round:

Sing the first verse of the song, **"Make New Friends,"** which goes, "Make new friends, but keep the old, one is silver and the other gold," together as a group 3x. Then divide the group into two sections and sing it as a two-part round. Possibly assign each section a group leader to help them come in on time and stay on their part. Be sure to cue each section when they need to start singing. Discuss Valentine's Day as a time to celebrate friendship as well as a time to celebrate love. Ask seniors to share about their best friends.

Shakers:

Pass out shakers and have the entire group shake in a high/low pattern to accentuate the rhythm of, **"Yes Sir, That's My Baby."** Practice keeping the rhythm steady and shaking on the beat together before singing. After singing with the shakers once, try singing it and shaking faster and faster!

Song Packets and Related Exercises:

Pass out song packets containing lyrics to all of the following songs to each group participant. Sing each song as a group and complete related exercises as indicated. See resources as needed.

NOTE: *I usually sing some, but not all of these, due to time.*

- **"What A Wonderful World"**
- **"Can't Help Falling in Love"**
- **"Fly Me to the Moon"**
- **"That's Amore"**– Prompt seniors to sing with extra enthusiasm!
- **"Skidamarink"**– Teach seniors choreographed hand movements to dance along.
- **"I Could Have Danced All Night"**
- **"Heart and Soul"**– Add hand bells to provide an accompaniment.
- **"Hey, Good Lookin'"**

Closing:

Lead a movement to music exercise with the Frank Sinatra recording, **"The Way You Look Tonight."** Give a variety of movement directions throughout the song. See Part Three for ideas.

ADDITIONAL RESOURCES:

Sweetheart/Valentine's Day Discussion Prompts

- What do we celebrate on Valentine's Day? (love, friendship)
- What are some ways of celebrating Valentine's Day? (parties, pink, red, and white decorations, chocolates, flowers, sending/receiving cards and valentines, making valentines, dancing, music)
- Tell me about your sweetheart! Did you marry him/her? How long were you married? What made your sweetheart special? (If additional prompts are needed, provide suggestions-funny, good looking, smart, caring, took care of you, etc.)

NOTE: *Some seniors can recall details and characteristics, but then get stuck on the name and become frustrated. Be prepared to support them and guide them to recalling and focusing on the positive details they do remember.*

"That's Amore"

Encourage seniors to really emphasize the phrase, "That's Amore" each time it is sung in the song! Have them practice energetically speaking the phrase a few times before singing the song to ensure maximum participation and enthusiasm.

"Skidamarink" Dance

There is a popular dance consisting entirely of hand movements to accompany this song. You can check out numerous variations on www.youtube.com. This is a great dance to perform while seated.

 ## "Heart and Soul" with Hand Bells

This is one of my favorite songs to do with the hand bells. It is a bit more challenging than others as the accompaniment moves at a faster tempo. Using a set of 20 chromatic hand bells, you will need four teams of two volunteers each to provide the chordal accompaniment to this song. The hand bells needed are:

1) G4 and B4
2) E4 and B3
3) A4 and C4
4) D4 and F#4

The accompaniment goes in this order throughout the entire song.

As a variation, rather than using hand bells to provide an accompaniment, I have also used drums and shakers to provide a rhythmic accompaniment. Have the drums play on beats 1 and 3 while the shakers play on beats 2-& and 4-&. The accompaniment would then be, Drum-shake, shake, Drum-shake, shake, though the rhythm of course should "swing" rather than be performed straight.

OUTLINE: *Favorite Foods*

Opening:

Pass out maracas, jingle bells, shakers, and tambourines being sure to give each senior a choice of what to play. Have seniors sing and shake along with several upbeat popular/favorite songs.

Introduce Theme:

Introduce today's theme of "Favorite Foods." It is surprising how many songs have been written about food. We usually think of songs focusing more on topics such as love, religion, patriotism, etc. but there are actually a surprising number of songs about food as well!

Movement to Music:

Lead a movement to music exercise with a recording of two songs, **"Bread and Butter"** and **"Tea for Two."** Suggested movements emphasizing work on the lower extremities are below.

- **"Bread and Butter"**– Tap toes, then tap heels, then alternate between tapping toes and heels (so the foot rocks back and forth). First have toes and heels tap at the same time, then have feet alternate (one foot taps toes while the other taps the heel, then reverse.) Move one foot out to the side then back into the center, then move the other foot out to the side and back into the center, keep alternating feet.

- **"Tea for Two"**– Move one foot out to the side then back into the center, then move the other foot out to the side and back into the center, keep alternating feet. Then move one foot forward, then back to center, then move it to the back and back to the center. Repeat with the opposite foot and complete several repetitions on each side. Finish by kicking with alternating legs.

Song Packets and Related Exercises:

Pass out song packets containing lyrics to all of the following songs to each group participant. Sing each song as a group and complete related exercises as indicated. See resources as needed.

- **"Jambalaya"**– Lead a brief discussion about favorite recipes. Discuss how jambalaya is made with a mixture of meat, veggies, and rice, but that there are many different variations and ways of making this dish. Ask seniors about their favorite dishes to cook or their favorite recipes. Also ask about who ate their cooking!

- **"Yes! We Have No Bananas"**– Ask seniors to list all of the different foods mentioned in the song.

- **"On the Good Ship Lollipop"**– Add hand bells to accompany and after singing, ask seniors to name all of the sweet treats mentioned in the song.

- **"Goober Peas"**– Add drums and cabasas to accompany after singing it through once first.

- **"My Favorite Things"**– Have seniors list their favorite foods. Possibly complete a songwriting exercise about favorite foods.

Drumming:

Pass out drums and a variety of percussion instruments and lead seniors in a drum circle.

Closing:

Lead the group in singing the song, **"Farewell Ladies, Farewell Gentlemen."**

ADDITIONAL RESOURCES:

"On the Good Ship Lollipop" with Hand Bells

See additional resources for the session, "Sun, Moon and Stars," for ideas and suggestions on introducing and using the hand bells to form chords to accompany a song.

This song works very well with the hand bells to provide a chordal accompaniment. The song contains mostly I and V chords, with a IV appearing only once, making for an easy to follow accompaniment pattern.

"Goober Peas"

This song has been around for a long time. In fact it was popular with Confederate soldiers during the Civil War. "Goober Peas" is another way of referring to boiled peanuts. After singing the song through as a group once, have some seniors play cabasas on the chorus to imitate the sound of cracking peanut shells, while other seniors play a strong, steady beat on the drums during the verses. After reviewing when each part plays, sing the song together again as a group with the added instrumental parts.

"My Favorite Things" Songwriting

This song could be used as the basis for a group songwriting activity about favorite foods.

_____ and _____
_____ and _____
_____ and _____ and _____ and _____

These are a few of our favorite foods!

_____ and _____
_____ and _____
_____ and _____ and _____ and _____

These are a few of our favorite foods!

When we eat (a food we don't like), When we eat (a food we don't like),

When the food gets burned

We simply remember our favorite foods

Then it doesn't taste so bad!

OUTLINE: *1930s*

Opening/Introduce Theme:

Lead seniors in singing along with one or two popular/favorite songs. Then introduce the theme of the 1930s.

Singing – "He's Got the Whole World in His Hands:"

Sing the song, "He's Got the Whole World in His Hands," together as a group. Have seniors take turns contributing ideas to place in the song. Seniors can decide to sing traditional verses or add in anything they choose. Provide options via prompt cards containing written suggestions or use verbal suggestions as needed to help seniors complete the phrase, "He's got _____ in His hands!"

Drums and Instruments:

Drum along with a recording of the song, "In the Mood." Keeping a steady beat, lead seniors to alternate between playing on the drumhead and on the rim, and between playing louder and softer. Shake small percussion instruments along with a recording of the song, "Stompin' at the Savoy." Direct seniors to shake along in a variety of ways with the rhythm of this piece. See Part Three for ideas.

Event Timeline:

Have seniors take turns drawing from an array of cue cards, each with a picture and/or description of an event of the 1930s to share with the group before placing the card in the appropriate place on a 1930s timeline.

Song Packets and Related Exercises:

Pass out song packets containing lyrics to all of the following songs to each group participant. Sing each song as a group and complete related exercises as indicated. See resources as needed.

NOTE: *I usually sing some, but not all of these, due to time.*

- "God Bless America" (1938)
- "I'm In the Mood for Love" (1935)
- "Blue Moon" (1934)
- "Heart and Soul" (1939)
- "Let's Call the Whole Thing Off" (1937)
- "Summertime" (Gershwin 1935)
- "Some Day My Prince Will Come" (from *Snow White* 1937) – Briefly discuss the plot and characters of the movie, *Snow White and the Seven Dwarfs*. It was the first full length feature animated cartoon, the first full length animated film produced by Walt Disney, and the first of its kind to be in full color.
- "Somewhere Over the Rainbow" (from *The Wizard of Oz* 1939) – Briefly discuss the plot and characters of the movie, *The Wizard of Oz*. It is now one of the most famous movies of all time, but it was also notable at the time of its release for its use of special effects and Technicolor!
- "I've Got Rhythm" (1930)

Group Songwriting:

After singing the song, "I've Got Rhythm," from the song packets, use that same tune and lead the group in a fill-in-the-blank style songwriting exercise about what they've got!

Closing:

Lead a movement to music exercise with a recording of the song, *"Bei Mir Bistu Shein."*

ADDITIONAL RESOURCES:

1930s Introduction

Briefly discuss how the 1930s were known as the time of the Great Depression following the stock market crash of 1929. However, the 30s produced some amazing music with jazz in the earlier part of the decade, and swing or "big band" music becoming popular in the second half of the decade. While we mostly associate big band music with the 30s, other songs became popular and significant in this era as well. President Herbert Hoover signed a congressional resolution in 1931 that officially made "The Star Spangled Banner" the national anthem of the United States. Marian Anderson, a famous singer who gained popularity in the 1930s, helped to break down racial barriers for African American artists. Among other things, she made the song, "He's Got the Whole World in His Hands," popular, a song which is still sung by all ages today!

Events of the 1930s

NOTE: *I usually do not do all of these due to time, but pick and choose based on the interests of the group.*

1930 Mickey Mouse makes his first appearance as a comic strip

1930 Hostess Twinkies are invented

1931 The "Star Spangled Banner" is adopted as the National Anthem of the United States

1931 The Empire State building is completed in New York City

1932 Radio City Music Hall opens in New York City

1933 *King Kong*, the original movie, premieres

1933 The 21st Amendment repeals Prohibition

1934 Clyde Barrow and Bonnie Parker, two infamous outlaws, are shot and killed

1935 Elvis Presley is born

1935 Babe Ruth plays his final game of baseball

1936 The Y.M.C.A. is founded

1936 The Hoover Dam opens

1937 The Golden Gate Bridge opens in San Francisco

1937 Walt Disney's movie, *Snow White and the Seven Dwarfs*, opens and becomes a smash hit

1938 Minimum wage is established by law in the USA

1939 Nazi Germany invades Poland, starting World War II

1939 The movie, *The Wizard of Oz*, is released

1939 The movie, *Gone with the Wind*, is released

"I've Got Rhythm" Songwriting

I've got_____ I've got_____

I've got my friends who could ask for anything more?

I've got_____ I've got_____

I've got my friends who could ask for anything more?

All my troubles, I don't mind them,

You won't find worry, 'round my door!

I've got_____ I've got_____

I've got my friends who could ask for anything more?

Who could ask for anything more?!

OUTLINE: *Weather*

NOTE: *This session works best in late winter/early spring, as seniors are often anticipating the coming of spring and better weather and a chance to get outside more often.*

Opening:

Lead seniors in singing along with three or four popular/favorite songs.

Introduce Theme/Group Discussion:

Introduce the theme of "Changing Weather." Discuss how changing weather is a sign of changing seasons. Ask seniors what different sorts of weather they have been observing.

Shakeable Instruments:

Pass out a variety of instruments and shake along with the following recorded songs.

- "Stormy Weather"– Lead seniors in playing with slow, rhythmic shakes, swaying side to side with the beat, doing two shakes to the right, then two shakes to the left, then to the right, etc.
- "Windy"– Lead seniors in shaking along by following different movement patterns. Start with shaking side to side as if doing the twist, then emphasize patterns using alternating hands. For example, shake with one hand high and one hand low, then switch. Shake with one arm stretched forward and one arm back towards the body, then switch, etc.

Song Packets and Related Exercises:

Pass out song packets containing lyrics to all of the following songs to each group participant. Sing each song as a group and complete related exercises as indicated. See resources as needed.

- "Singin' in the Rain"
- "Oh, What A Beautiful Morning"
- "I'm Looking Over a Four Leaf Clover" – Add hand bells to represent each "leaf."
- "Button Up Your Overcoat"– Add instrumental sound effects to the chorus.
- "Raindrops Keep Fallin' On My Head"
- "Somewhere Over the Rainbow"– Discuss what weather conditions create a rainbow.

Closing:

Lead the group in singing the song, "Happy Trails," 2x.

ADDITIONAL RESOURCES:

"I'm Looking Over A Four Leaf Clover"

After singing through the song once, ask seniors to recall what each of the four leaves represent according to the song lyrics. Ask for volunteers to musically represent each "leaf" using the hand bells. Use a prompt card for each leaf to help each senior/group of seniors to remember when to play. If the song is performed in the key of "C," the following hand bells will be used.

- **Sunshine (G, B)**
- **Rain (A, C#)**
- **Roses (D)**
- **Somebody I Adore (D, F#)**

Give seniors a chance to practice playing at the appropriate time, then sing the song as a group 2x with the hand bells musically highlighting each "leaf" of the clover!

Rainbows

If it's been a while since science class, remember that rainbows can be seen when there are water drops in the air and sunlight is shining from behind them, specifically at a low angle. So if it's raining and sunny, especially in the late afternoon or early morning, it's a great time to look for a rainbow. Rainbows appear opposite the sun, from the observer's perspective.

"Button Up Your Overcoat"

Add instrumental and vocal parts to highlight the chorus of the song, which goes as follows:

"Button up your overcoat,
When the wind is free,
Take good care of yourself,
You belong to me!"

Divide the entire group into four sections. Section one will shake the jingle bells on the words, "Button up your overcoat," Section two will play the slide whistles on the words, "When the wind is free," Section three will shout: "Take good care of yourself," Section four will respond: "You belong to me!"

Then sing the entire song as a group with the instrumental and vocal parts highlighting the lyrics of the chorus, each time the chorus is repeated.

For more advanced groups, divide the group into two sections only. The first section will play the bells on the words, "Button up your overcoat," and later shout: "Take good care of yourself." The second section will play the slide whistles on the words, "When the wind is free," and later respond, "You belong to me!"

OUTLINE: *Saint Patrick's Day*

Opening/Introduce Theme:

Lead seniors in singing along with a few popular/favorite songs. Then introduce the theme of "Saint Patrick's Day."

Drumming:

Pass out drums and a variety of percussion instruments and lead seniors in a drum circle.

Movement to Music:

Play two recorded songs and lead seniors in two movement to music exercises while seated.

- **"Irish Washerwoman"** – Place hands on hips thinking about imitating Irish dancing, then tap toes, march in place, kick alternating legs, etc.
- **"Whiskey in the Jar"** – Start with clapping, then pat knees, then alternate between patting knees and clapping, then alternate between patting knees and tapping shoulders, then pat knees and tap alternating shoulders crossing midline, finish with tapping toes and clapping.

Group Discussion:

Discuss the history of Saint Patrick's Day, things that are Irish, ways to celebrate the holiday, etc. Use pictures as prompts as needed.

Song Packets and Related Exercises:

Pass out song packets containing lyrics to all of the following songs to each group participant. Sing each song as a group.

- "I'm Looking Over a Four Leaf Clover"
- "Danny Boy"
- "An Irish Lullaby"
- "When Irish Eyes are Smiling"

Singing/Drumming:

As Saint Patrick's Day is often celebrated with a drink, sing the song, **"There's A Tavern in the Town."** First have seniors add a steady drumbeat to accompany. Then teach seniors a long-short-short (think quarter note, eighth note, eighth note) drumbeat pattern and have them play it while singing again. Speed the song up and perform it faster and faster!

Shakeable Instruments:

Pass out a variety of instruments and have seniors shake along with two recorded songs by Gaelic Storm, **"Born to Be A Bachelor"** and **"Punjab Paddy."** Direct seniors to shake along in a variety of ways with the rhythm of these songs. See Part Three for ideas.

Closing:

Lead seniors in a variety of movements to dance along with a recording of the song, **"I Miss My Home,"** by Gaelic Storm.

ADDITIONAL RESOURCES:

 History of Saint Patrick's Day/Irish Group Discussion Ideas:

NOTE: *I like to use pictures of the Irish countryside and coast, the Irish Flag, the Blarney Stone, clovers, leprechauns, etc. to help guide the discussion as well.*

History of the Holiday:

- Saint Patrick's Day is celebrated each year on March 17th.
- Saint Patrick is the patron saint of Ireland and is one of the most celebrated religious figures around the world.
- Saint Patrick was a priest and a Christian missionary to Ireland and is credited with bringing the written word (the Bible) to the Irish people.
- Though there were a few Christians living in Ireland, Saint Patrick is credited with bringing about a massive religious change from paganism to Christianity, and laying the groundwork for the start of hundreds of monasteries and churches.
- It is believed that Saint Patrick died on March 17th in the fifth century.
- America celebrated its first Saint Patrick's Day in Boston in 1737.
- Over 100 US cities now hold Saint Patrick's Day parades.
- On Saint Patrick's Day it is often said that, "Everyone is Irish," meaning that everyone can celebrate and enjoy the holiday.

Other Fun Facts:

- According to the 2010 U.S. census, over 34 million Americans have Irish ancestry.
- According to the *Guinness Book of World Records*, the highest number of leaves ever found on a clover is 14.
- The Blarney Stone is a block of Bluestone built into Blarney Castle in 1446. According to legend, kissing the blarney stone gives the kisser the "gift of gab" or eloquent speech.

Examples of Ways to Celebrate the Holiday:

- Drinking Beer
- Parades
- Wearing Green
- Eating Corned Beef and Cabbage
- Pinching Those Not Wearing Green
- Listening to Irish Music
- Family or Community Traditions

OUTLINE: *Folk Songs* I

Opening:

Pass out drums and a variety of percussion instruments and lead seniors in a short drum circle.

Introduce Theme:

Introduce today's theme of "American Folk Songs." Discuss how folk songs are an important part of our culture and how they represent different periods of history and different geographical locations. Folk songs are a way of capturing and preserving our national identity and passing it down from generation to generation. In fact, folk songs are enjoyed and sung by all ages, from small children in preschool to grandparents and great-grandparents.

Song Packets and Related Exercises:

Pass out song packets containing lyrics to all of the following songs to each group participant. Sing each song as a group and complete related exercises as indicated. See resources as needed.

- "Oh Susanna"
- "My Bonnie Lies Over the Ocean"– Have seniors take turns providing an accompaniment on the ocean drum(s) during the different verses. Or have seniors sway side to side with the rhythm of the song, which emulates the feeling of the ocean.
- "The Erie Canal Song"
- "Home on the Range"– Discuss "home" after singing.
- "Down By the Riverside"

Group Songwriting:

After singing the song, "Down By the Riverside," from the song packets, use the tune and lead the group in a fill-in-the-blank style songwriting exercise about favorite community activities.

Singing – "He's Got the Whole World in His Hands":

Sing the song, "He's Got the Whole World in His Hands," together as a group. Have seniors take turns contributing ideas to place in the song. Seniors can decide to sing traditional verses or add in anything they choose. Provide options via prompt cards containing written suggestions or use verbal suggestions as needed to help seniors complete the phrase, "He's got_____in His hands!"

Singing in a Round:

Sing the song, "Row, Row, Row Your Boat," together as a group 2x. Then divide the group into three sections and sing it as a three part round. Possibly assign each section a group leader to help them come in on time and stay on their part. Be sure to cue each section when they need to start singing.

Closing:

Lead the group in singing the song, "Happy Trails," 2x.

ADDITIONAL RESOURCES:

"Home" Group Discussion Prompts

After singing the song, "Home on the Range," discuss the concept of "home." Ask seniors what the author of this song says about his home (skies are never cloudy, breezes are balmy and light, the air is pure, seldom hear a discouraging word, the deer and the antelope are at play, etc.) Does the author like his home? Folk songs are about a shared home here in America. What are some great things about calling America "home?" What makes a place a "home?" Describe your home. (Seniors could describe their childhood homes, maybe the home where they raised their family, etc.) What made your home special? What about your home now? What are some things that make this community feel like home? What are some things that make this community special?

"Down By the Riverside" Songwriting

As a group complete several verses of the following song,
sung to the first part of the tune of "Down By the Riverside."

We like to _____

Down here at ___(Name of retirement community or day program)___

Down here at ___(Name of retirement community or day program)___

Down here at ___(Name of retirement community or day program)___

We like to _____

Down here at ___(Name of retirement community or day program)___

And have fun with our friends all day!

OUTLINE: *Folk Songs* II

Opening:

Review the significance of "folk songs" as discussed in the previous session. Lead seniors in singing a few of the more popular folk songs sung in the previous session such as **"Oh Susanna," "My Bonnie Lies Over the Ocean,"** and **"Home on the Range."**

Movement to Music:

Have the group sing-along and move as you play and sing, **"When the Saints Go Marching In."** Add a different movement direction to move with the beat every two verses.

NOTE: *For smaller groups, have seniors take turns playing the chords on the xylophone during different verses. Remove the extra bars and provide assistance as needed.*

Song Packets and Related Exercises:

Pass out song packets containing lyrics to all of the following songs to each group participant. Sing each song as a group and complete related exercises as indicated. See resources as needed.

- **"Camptown Races"** – Sing the 'doo-dah' part in a call and response style. The therapist sings and then the group echoes back. Encourage loud and enthusiastic participation! Practice the call and response part first, then sing the entire song.
- **"Polly-Wolly-Doodle"**
- **"Clementine"**
- **"Billy Boy"**
- **"Old Folks at Home"**

Instrumental Performance:

Refresh everyone's memory of the song, **"She'll Be Coming 'Round the Mountain,"** by singing the first verse as a group. Then verbally review all of the different verses. Use a different instrument to create sound effects for each different verse. Ask for volunteer(s) to 'solo' on each verse and allow them to choose an instrument to play to represent their verse. Each of the six verses will have different instrumental sound effects and different volunteer(s) performing. Practice following cues to start and stop playing and then sing the entire song as a group with the different instrumental sound effects throughout.

Hand Bells:

Use the hand bells to create a chordal accompaniment for the song, **"This Little Light of Mine."** Sing the song as a group with the hand bells playing on cue to provide the accompaniment.

Closing:

Pass out drums. Lead everyone to play together on a steady beat. Maintain this steady beat as the group sings, **"I've Been Working on the Railroad."** Then change the drum pattern to a long-short-long (think dotted quarter note, eighth note, dotted quarter, etc.) and have seniors drum the new pattern while singing the song again.

Pass out additional drums and other percussion instruments as needed and lead seniors in a drum circle.

ADDITIONAL RESOURCES:

"When the Saints Go Marching In" Movement to Music

"Oh, When the saints go marching in..." etc. **Tap Toes**

"Oh, When the sun begins to shine..." etc. **Tap Toes**

"Oh, When the saints go marching in..." etc. **March In Place**

"Oh, When the choir begins to sing...." etc. **March in Place**

"Oh, When the saints go marching in..." etc. **Pat Knees**

"Oh, When the preacher begins to preach..." etc. **Pat Knees**

"Oh, When the saints go marching in..." etc. **Clap Hands**

"Oh, When the trumpet begins to sound..." etc. **Clap Hands**

"Oh, When the saints go marching in..." etc.(2x) **Clap and March in Place**

She'll Be Coming 'Round the Mountain

I like to use the following verses:

"She'll be comin' round the mountain..."

"We'll all go out to meet her...."

"We'll kill the old red rooster...."

"We'll all have chicken and dumplings....."

"She'll be wearing red pajamas...."

"She will have (I modify "have" to "get") to sleep with Grandma..."

"This Little Light of Mine" with Hand Bells

See additional resources for the session, "Sun, Moon and Stars," for ideas and suggestions on introducing and using the hand bells to form chords to accompany a song.

This is a great song to use hand bells to accompany. It can either be performed with three chords (I, IV, V) or four if you want to add in a vi chord as well.

OUTLINE: *Springtime/Easter*

Opening/Introduce Theme:

Lead seniors in singing along with three or four popular/favorite songs. Then introduce the theme of "Springtime."

Maracas and Shakers:

Pass out maracas and shakers and lead seniors in shaking along with a recording of the song, **"Spring Fever,"** by Elvis Presley. The song is short, so do it 2x. Briefly model various rhythmic shaking patterns for seniors to follow and then ask each senior to demonstrate a way to shake along for the group to imitate.

Movement to Music:

Lead seniors in a low-key movement to music exercise with a recording of the song, **"April in Paris."**

Suggested Movements: Sway side to side, tap toes, kicks with alternating feet, swing arms with the beat, shoulder shrugs, etc.

Song Packets and Related Exercises (Part 1):

Pass out song packets containing lyrics to all of the following songs to each group participant. Lead seniors in a discussion about springtime, in between singing the following springtime songs as a group.

NOTE: *I usually sing some, but not all of these, due to time.*

- "Oh, What a Beautiful Morning"
- "Blue Skies"
- "I'm Looking Over a Four Leaf Clover"
- "Singin' in the Rain"
- "What A Wonderful World"
- "Zip-A-Dee-Doo-Dah"

Group Songwriting:

Lead the group in a fill-in-the-blank style songwriting exercise about favorite springtime activities and things that remind them of springtime to the tune of **"Summertime"** by George Gershwin.

Group Discussion:

Lead seniors in a discussion about Easter.

Modified Bunny Hop:

Teach seniors a modified version of **"The Bunny Hop"** that can be danced while seated. After a quick review of the movements, put on a recording of the song and lead seniors in dancing along.

Song Packets (Part 2):

- **"The Easter Parade"**
- **"Here Comes Peter Cottontail"**

Closing:

Lead the group in singing the song, **"Old Time Religion,"** and/or **"I Saw the Light."**

Encourage seniors to clap along and/or tap their toes with these two lively songs.

ADDITIONAL RESOURCES:

Springtime Discussion Prompts

What sort of things come to mind when you think about springtime? What sort of changes do we see in the weather? What are some fun things to do in the spring? (picnics, walks outside, flying a kite, going fishing, gardening, camping, etc.) What holidays do we celebrate in the spring? (Saint Patrick's Day, Easter, Mother's Day, *Cinco de Mayo*, Memorial Day, etc.)

Springtime Songwriting

To the tune of "Summertime" by George Gershwin

Springtime, and the livin' is easy

_____and_____

We like to_____and_____and_____

We're happy dear friends, it's springtime!

Complete the first two blanks by asking seniors what they think about when they think about springtime. Common responses include: the flowers are blooming, the birds are singing, the grass grows green, the days are sunny, etc. Complete the rest of the blanks with favorite springtime activities, referencing the discussion from earlier in the session. Write two verses if the group is feeling inspired!

Easter Discussion Prompts

Which of the following prompts you use will depend very much on the demographic of the group with which you are working. Many of my senior groups are very religious and excited to talk about the meaning of Easter. Use your judgement when steering the conversation.

Why do we celebrate Easter? What are some ways of celebrating Easter? (going to church, wearing a new dress and hat, decorating with flowers/Easter lilies, seeing family, eating a big Easter dinner, Easter baskets and candy, Easter egg hunt, children waiting for the Easter bunny, etc.)

Modified "Bunny Hop"

This version of the "Bunny Hop" dance is very similar to the original. Complete the following sequence of movements with each verse. These steps very closely match the steps indicated in the lyrics of the song, but the "hops" are replaced with stomps.

- Kick Right foot out 2x
- Kick Left foot out 2x
- Kick Right foot out 2x
- Stomp, Stomp, Stomp

OUTLINE: *Friendship*

Opening:

Lead seniors in singing along with several popular/favorite songs. Include a few slower songs and plenty of upbeat songs.

Introduce Theme/Movement to Music:

Introduce today's theme of "Friendship" and lead a movement to music exercise with a recording of the song, **"Stand by Me."** Have seniors hold hands for the duration of the song and alternate between swaying side to side together as a group and swinging their arms forwards and backwards as a group.

Song Packets and Related Exercises:

Pass out song packets containing lyrics to all of the following songs to each group participant. Sing each song as a group and complete related exercises as indicated. See resources as needed.

- **"Side By Side"**– Add drums to accompany the song, either with a steady beat or with a long-short-long-short pattern (think dotted quarter note-eighth note but swinging the rhythm).
- **"Getting to Know You"**– After singing the song, discuss how to make new friends.
- **"It's a Small World"**– Sing through once, then add hand bells, forming chords, to accompany.

- **"Lean on Me"**– Discuss important qualities in a friend and/or have seniors share about their best friends.
- **"Vive La Compagnie"**– Before singing, teach seniors the chorus of this song. Practice speaking the words in a call and response style (the therapist speaks a line, then seniors repeat it). Encourage strong articulation and emphatic phrasing of the chorus.

Singing in a Round:

Sing the first verse of the song, **"Make New Friends,"** which goes, "Make new friends, but keep the old, one is silver and the other gold," together as a group 3x. Then divide the group into two sections and sing it as a two part round. Possibly assign each section a group leader to help them come in on time and stay on their part. Be sure to cue each section when they need to start singing.

Maracas and Shakers:

Pass out maracas and shakers and have seniors shake along with a recording of the song, **"With A Little Help from My Friends."** Emphasizing the rhythm of the song, shake high and low, and side to side.

Closing:

Pass out drums and a variety of percussion instruments and lead seniors in a drum circle.

ADDITIONAL RESOURCES:

"Getting to Know You" Discussion Prompts

How do you get to know someone? (say hello, introduce yourself, ask about their interests, spend time together, etc.) What are some ways to meet new friends? What are some ways you can meet new friends here at this community? (attend activities and programs offered, sit with someone new at lunch or dinner, smile, encourage other residents to attend one of the activities with you, just introduce yourself and strike up a conversation!)

"Lean on Me" Discussion Prompts

What do you look for in a good friend? What are some important qualities of a friend? (trustworthy, positive/cheerful, encouraging, good listener, shared interests, fun, caring, is there for you, puts others first, shared sense of humor, etc.)

Ask seniors about their best friends from grade school, friends they had as adults, friends they have here at their community, etc. Ask about how long they have been friends with that person, what they have in common, why they consider that individual a best friend, etc.

 Introducing and Using the Hand Bells

See additional resources for the session, "Sun, Moon and Stars," for ideas and suggestions on introducing and using the hand bells to form chords to accompany a song.

"It's a Small World" only requires three different chords, D, A, and G, and is generally a fairly easy accompaniment pattern to follow on the hand bells!

OUTLINE: *Fiesta*

Opening:

Lead seniors in singing along with several popular/favorite songs.

Introduce Theme/Group Discussion:

Introduce today's theme of "Fiesta," reminding seniors that the word, "fiesta," means party! Lead a discussion about Mexico and/or *Cinco De Mayo.*

Movement to Music:

Play a recording of the song, *"Cielito Lindo."* Prompt seniors to hold hands and sway side to side as a group with the music and then swing their arms forwards and backwards as a group. Add in a few kicks as well with alternating legs.

Maracas and Shakers:

Pass out maracas and shakers to shake and dance along with several recorded songs. Possible song choices include: *"La Cucaracha," "Fiesta," "Guantanamera,"* and *"Tequila."*

You could give directions to shake along in a variety of ways with the rhythm of these songs. However, from my experience, most seniors automatically respond to music this lively and start moving and dancing in their own creative ways!

Song Packets and Related Exercises:

Pass out song packets containing lyrics to all of the following songs to each group participant. Sing each song as a group and complete related exercises as indicated. See resources as needed.

- *"La Bamba"*– Teach seniors the phrase, "la la la bamba," and have them practice saying it several times before singing the song straight through. Though they may not know Spanish, EVERYONE can sing the repeating "la la la bamba" lines. Practice with them in a call and response style (therapist speaks, then seniors repeat) encouraging them to say it louder and louder and with more enthusiasm. Encourage them to shout it loudly and enthusiastically as everyone sings the song together 2-3x.

- *"De Colores"*– Summarize the translation of the lyrics and explain the meaning of the song before singing it as a group.

- *"Mi Cuerpo"*– Give the translation of the lyrics before singing it through 2x. Then add the movements indicated in the song and try the whole song several times with the movements, going faster and faster with each repetition!

Modified Mexican Hat Dance:

Teach choreographed movements to the **"Mexican Hat Dance"** and then perform the dance as a group along with a recording of the song.

Closing:

Pass out drums and a variety of percussion instruments and lead seniors in a drum circle, if there is time. If out of time, lead the group in singing the song, **"Farewell Ladies, Farewell Gentlemen."**

ADDITIONAL RESOURCES:

 Mexico/Cinco De Mayo Group Discussion Ideas

About Cinco de Mayo:

- *Cinco de Mayo* is celebrated on the 5th of May.
- This holiday does NOT celebrate Mexico's independence from Spain.
- In 1862, the French invaded Mexico. In the Battle of Pueblo, General Ignacio Zaragoza's army of about 4,000 soldiers defeated a French army of twice that size. Though the French continued to occupy Mexico until 1866, the soldiers' courage and determination was an inspiration to many, including many Mexican Americans.
- The story was popularized in America during the 1960s and 1970s, turning it into a popular holiday.
- You do not have to be Mexican to celebrate!

About Mexico/Mexican Culture:

I like to use pictures to aid in the discussion. I usually start with a map and we discuss where Mexico is located in relation to the United States. Then we discuss some of the things unique to Mexican culture, such as examples of Mexican food, sombreros, piñatas, siestas, fiestas, bright colors, outdoor markets, etc.

"Mi Cuerpo" and Dance

"*Mi Cuerpo, mi cuerpo hace musica*	"My body makes music, it's easy you will see
Mi Cuerpo, mi cuerpo hace musica	My body makes music, it's easy you will see
Mis manos hacen 'clap, clap, clap'	My hands, my hands go 'clap, clap, clap'
Mis pies hacen 'tap, tap, tap'	My feet, my feet go 'tap, tap, tap'
Mi boca hace 'la, la, la'	My mouth, my mouth goes 'la, la, la'
Mi cuerpo hace cha, cha-cha!"	My body does the cha-cha-cha!"

Have everyone clap hands on "clap, clap, clap," tap their toes on "tap, tap, tap," sing with the "la, la, las," and shake shoulders with the "cha-cha-chas." While I give the English translation, I usually only sing the Spanish version with my groups. We practice it a few times to help the seniors remember the sequence of movements without the English words to prompt them.

Modified Mexican Hat Dance

NOTE: *I use an instrumental version that is not too fast.*

Kick, Kick, Kick, Clap Clap, Kick, Kick, Kick, Clap Clap (2x with the beat of the chorus). On verses roll arms, and then roll arms in the opposite direction.

OUTLINE: *Television & Movies*

Opening/Introduce Theme:

Lead seniors in singing along with no more than one or two popular/favorite songs. Then introduce the theme of music from famous television shows and the movies.

Shakeable Instruments:

Pass out a variety of instruments and shake along with recordings of several famous television theme songs. Have seniors identify which television show the song is from. Theme songs to use include: **"Batman," "Gilligan's Island," "I Love Lucy,"** and **"The Beverly Hillbillies."**

Movement to Music:

Play a recording of the theme song from **"Bonanza"** and have seniors identify which television show the song is from, before leading a movement to music exercise. Give a variety of movement directions throughout the song. See Part Three for ideas.

Boomwhackers:

Introduce the Boomwhackers and encourage seniors to try them out. Then use the boomwhackers to play along with a recording of **"The Andy Griffith Show"** theme song and **"The Addams Family"** theme song. Play a bit of each theme song first, just long enough for seniors to identify the television show associated with the theme songs, before playing along.

Song Packets and Related Exercises:

Pass out song packets containing lyrics to all of the following songs to each group participant. Sing each song as a group and then have seniors identify what movie each song is from. I use pictures of movie posters to narrow their options and help with recall. Have seniors briefly discuss the plot, name famous actors and actresses in the film, describe the film's setting etc. I usually do not get through all of these due to time, but pick and choose which ones to do based upon the group. See resources as needed.

- **"Take Me Out to the Movies"** (Song Parody) – Sing and discuss favorite genres of film.
- **"As Time Goes By"** (*Casablanca*)
- **"Singin' in the Rain"** (*Singin' in the Rain*)
- **"When You Wish Upon a Star"** (*Pinocchio*)
- **"I Could Have Danced All Night"** (*My Fair Lady*)
- **"My Own True Love"** (*Gone With the Wind*) *The original piece had no lyrics, however the melody is the same.
- **"Somewhere Over the Rainbow"** (*The Wizard of Oz*)
- **"Someday My Prince Will Come"** (*Snow White*)
- **"My Favorite Things"** (*The Sound of Music*)
- **"Do-Re-Mi"** (*The Sound of Music*)

Closing:

Teach choreographed movements to the song, **"Supercalifragilisticexpialidocious,"** (from the movie, *Mary Poppins*). Practice the sequence 2x and then dance along with a recording of the song.

ADDITIONAL RESOURCES:

Boomwhackers:

For ideas on how to introduce the boom-whackers, see the "Halloween" session additional resources.

"The Andy Griffith Show" Theme – Have seniors play along by keeping a steady beat. With higher functioning groups, have seniors alternate between playing their set of boomwhackers alone, and playing with a neighbor.

"The Addams Family" Theme – Hum the melody of the chorus and have seniors prac-tice playing the boomwhackers in place of the finger snaps in the song. Practice the chorus reminding them to wait on the third line for the two hits. Practice keeping a steady beat during the verses. Once seniors seem comfortable with this pattern, put on the recording and play along, keeping a steady beat on the verses and playing where the finger snaps occur in the chorus.

"Take Me Out to the Movies" (To the tune of "Take Me Out to the Ballgame")

This song is NOT meant to be a songwriting exercise, rather it is included in the song packets.

Take me out to the movies,

Take me out with the crowd.

Buy me some popcorn and soda pop,

I want the good times to never stop!

Let me sit and watch on the big screen,

The picture seems so real

So please take me out to the movies,

to see the film!

"Supercalifragilisticexpialidocious" Choreographed Dance

Chorus ("Supercalifragilisticexpialidocious..." etc) ~ Tap Toes with the beat

Bridge ("Um diddle diddle diddle um diddle ay..." etc.) ~ Roll Arms

Verses ~ Clap Hands with the beat

OUTLINE: *Patriotic*

Opening:

Pass out a variety of small percussion instruments and lead seniors in singing and shaking along with a couple upbeat popular/favorite songs.

Introduce Theme/Group Discussion:

This session works best in conjunction with a patriotic holiday such as Memorial Day, Veteran's Day or Independence Day. Ask seniors about the holiday coming up, why we observe it and ways of observing/celebrating the holiday. Review and discuss the history and significance of that particular patriotic holiday.

Lyric Discussion:

Lead seniors in singing the song, **"Don't Sit Under the Apple Tree."** Discuss the meaning of the lyrics and history. This song became famous during World War II. The lyrics describe a young man going off to war and asking his sweetheart to remain faithful until his return.

NOTE: *If you work with seniors, no doubt you've sung this song a hundred times, but did you know the Dinning Sisters wrote a parody response? It's titled, "They Just Chopped Down the Old Apple Tree."*

Movement to Music:

Play a recording of the march, **"Stars and Stripes Forever,"** and lead seniors in marching, moving, and clapping along with the beat.

Song Packets and Related Exercises/Name That Tune:

Pass out song packets containing lyrics to all of the following songs to each group participant.

Listen to an instrumental version of each of the following songs and ask seniors to identify the song. Then sing the song together as a group. Also, have seniors identify the following tunes without singing them afterwards: **"Hail to the Chief," "Taps," "Reveille."**

- **"America"** (**"My Country 'Tis of Thee"**)
- **"America the Beautiful"**
- **"Battle Hymn of the Republic"**
- **"God Bless America"**
- **"Star-Spangled Banner"**
- **"Yankee Doodle"**
- **"Yankee Doodle Boy"**
- **"You're A Grand Old Flag"**

Drumming:

Pass out drums and a variety of percussion instruments and lead seniors in playing along with a recording of **"The Washington Post March,"** playing louder and softer with the music.

Closing:

Lead seniors in a drum circle, if there is time. Otherwise close with the above drumming exercise.

ADDITIONAL RESOURCES:

 Patriotic Holiday Quick Facts

MEMORIAL DAY: Initially known as Decoration Day, Memorial Day honors and remembers those who have died in our nation's service. There are several stories about how the holiday came to be and most likely it started as separate holidays in a variety of towns as a way to honor those who had died in war. Memorial Day was first observed on May 30, 1868, when flowers were placed on the graves of soldiers (both Union and Confederate) in Arlington National Cemetery. The holiday was observed by all of the Northern states by 1890. The South refused to recognize the day, maintaining separate days to honor their dead until the end of World War I, when the holiday came to honor all those who had died in any war. It is now celebrated nationally, after officially being established by Congress with the National Holiday Act of 1971, and is observed on the last Monday in May.

JULY 4TH/INDEPENDENCE DAY: America existed back in the 1700s as a collection of British colonies, under the rule of the British government. In 1763, Britain decided to exert more control over the colonies, which included paying taxes and paying for the defense of the colonies by the British army. The colonists were frustrated at being made to pay taxes when they were not represented in the British Parliament, hence the well-known phrase, "no taxation without representation." The colonists formed the First Continental Congress in an attempt to prompt the British government to recognize their rights. When the attempt failed, the American Revolution started. During the American Revolution, a Second Continental Congress was formed which adopted a final draft of the Declaration of Independence. The Declaration of Independence was formally adopted on July 4, 1776. Even though Americans had declared themselves to be independent from Britain, the American Revolution was still being fought and did not come to a victorious end until 1783.

VETERANS DAY: Veteran Day is observed each year on November 11th. It is a holiday to celebrate and honor all of America's veterans, their dedication to this country, and their willingness to serve and protect it. In November 1919, President Wilson declared November 11th to be the first commemoration of Armistice Day. Armistice Day celebrated the end of World War I, which at the time was thought to be the "war to end all wars." Later in 1954, after World War II and the Korean War, Armistice Day was changed to Veterans Day in order to honor American veterans of all wars.

Common Ways of Observing Patriotic Holidays:

- Parades
- Memorial Services
- Placing Flowers on the Graves of Fallen Soldiers
- Thanking a Veteran
- Fireworks
- Firecrackers
- Picnics
- Barbeques
- Family Get-Togethers
- Displaying Flags
- Decorating with Red, White, and Blue

OUTLINE: *Summer*

Opening/Introduce Theme:

Lead seniors in singing along with several popular/favorite songs. Then introduce the theme of "Summertime."

Movement to Music:

Lead a movement to music exercise with a recording of the song, **"Lazy, Hazy, Crazy, Days of Summer."** Give a variety of movement directions throughout the song. See Part Three for ideas.

Group Discussion/Singing:

Lead a brief group discussion about favorite summertime activities and lead into the next two songs.

- **"Take Me Out to the Ballgame"** – Sing and discuss baseball including what positions seniors played when they were young, what teams seniors are currently watching, the number of innings in a game, the food served at baseball games, etc.
- **"Bicycle Built for Two"**

Maracas and Shakers:

Pass out maracas and shakers and have seniors shake along with two recorded songs, **"Summertime Blues"** and **"Surf City."** Direct seniors to shake along in a variety of ways with the rhythm of these songs. See Part Three for ideas.

Song Packets and Related Exercises:

Pass out song packets containing lyrics to all of the following songs to each group participant. Sing each song as a group and complete related exercises as indicated. See resources as needed.

- **"Ain't We Got Fun"**
- **"Summertime"** (Gershwin) – Discuss, demonstrate, and practice healthy breathing techniques before singing these long phrases!
- **"In the Good Old Summertime"** – Add hand bells to create a "G" chord and have seniors (ask for volunteers/select volunteers) play the bells on the word, "Summertime," every time it appears in the song. First practice playing each time the word is spoken by the therapist, then play each time the word occurs in the context of the song, as the group sings the song 2x. Do a fill-in-the-blank style songwriting exercise with the song, "In the Good Old Summertime," asking seniors to work together to choose ideas to place in the song. Rotate the hand bells to other seniors in the group. Instruct them to again play every time the group sings the word, "summertime." Sing through the group's new song 2x with the hand bells still playing every time the word, "summertime," is sung.
- **"Under the Boardwalk"** – Have seniors play the shakers along with this song to create the sound of the beach!
- **"Zip-A-Dee-Doo-Dah"**

Closing:

Lead the group in singing the song, **"Farewell Ladies, Farewell Gentlemen."**

ADDITIONAL RESOURCES:

Summertime Things and Ideas

For use in the group discussion and the songwriting exercise.

- Baseball
- Fishing
- Camping
- Vacations
- The Beach
- Picnics
- Taking a Walk
- Barbeques

- Gardening
- Flying a Kite
- Ice Cream (and favorite flavors!)
- Watermelon
- Swimming
- Iced Tea
- Cold Beer (Yes, seniors are all of age and this is a popular response!)

Summertime Songwriting

To the tune of "In the Good Old Summertime"

In the good old summertime, In the good old summertime,

We like to _____ and _____ and _____,

Having such a good time!

We think of _____ and _____ and _____,

And that's a very good sign,

That we'll all have fun together in, the good old summertime!

OUTLINE: *Travel*

Opening/Introduce Theme:

Lead seniors in singing along with several popular/favorite songs. Pass out bells and shake along with **"Jingle Jangle Jingle."** Then introduce the theme of "Travel."

Movement to Music:

Lead a movement to music exercise with a recording of the song, **"New York, New York,"** by Frank Sinatra. Think of "chorus line" moves and switch between chorus line kicks with alternating legs and swaying side to side with accentuated shoulder movements.

Song Packets and Related Exercises:

Pass out song packets containing lyrics to all of the following songs to each group participant. Sing each song as a group and complete related exercises as indicated. See resources as needed.

- **"Side By Side"** – Have seniors share about their favorite travel companions.
- **"You Belong to Me"** – Identify travel destinations indicated and described in the song.
- **"Sentimental Journey"** – Have seniors share memories of favorite trips they have taken.

- **"Bye, Bye, Blackbird"**
- **"It's a Small World"** – Add hand bells, forming chords, to accompany.
- **"Take Me Home, Country Roads"** – Discuss how coming home can also be a good part of traveling.

Group Songwriting:

Work as a group to write multiple verses of a song about traveling to the tune of **"She'll Be Coming 'Round the Mountain."** Include places seniors have visited or would like to visit and how they would travel to get there.

Music Listening/Movement/Group Discussion:

While listening to examples of music from around the world, have seniors pass or toss a ball around the group until the music stops (like musical chairs). The senior holding the ball when the music stops either (a) describes a place they once visited on a trip or (b) draws a card with a picture and some facts about a travel destination to share with the group. I like to include some fairly local places, some U.S. destinations, and some destinations from other continents.

Closing:

Lead the group in singing the song, **"Happy Trails."**

ADDITIONAL RESOURCES:

Travel Songwriting
To the tune of "She'll Be Coming 'Round the Mountain"

Oh we'd like to go to _____ on(in) a _____ ,

Oh we'd like to go to _____ on(in) a _____ ,

Oh we'd like to go to _____ , yes we'd like to go to _____ ,

Oh we'd like to go to _____ on(in) a _____ !

For example, "We'd like to go to China on a boat," or "We'd like to go to the Grand Canyon on a horse." etc. I usually sing multiple versions of this song with my seniors, using a different location and mode of travel each time. It also gives many people a chance to write a verse and share their ideas.

 Introducing and Using the Hand Bells

See additional resources for the session, "Sun, Moon and Stars," for ideas and suggestions on introducing and using the hand bells to form chords to accompany a song.

"It's a Small World" only requires three different chords, D, A, and G, and is generally a fairly easy accompaniment pattern to follow with the hand bells!

OUTLINE: *United States*

Opening:

Lead seniors in singing along with three or four popular/favorite songs.

Introduce Theme/Group Discussion:

Introduce today's theme of the "United States." Discuss how America is different from other countries in that we have a state identity in addition to a national identity. We tend to identify ourselves as being "American" but also as being a "Texan," or a "New Yorker," a "Californian," etc. Here in America we can have both national pride and state pride. Ask seniors which states they are from and what makes that state unique or special. Ask them what other states they have lived in or visited and what was special or memorable about those locations as well.

Drumming:

Lead seniors in drumming along with a recording of a patriotic march, such as **"The Washington Post March."** Drum along with the dynamics of the march and lead seniors in different techniques such as "rim shots" on the hard edge (rim) of the drum, louder hits on the center of the drumhead, and softer taps on the edge of the drumhead.

Lead seniors in a brief drum circle (approximately 10 minutes).

Song Packets and Related Exercises:

Pass out song packets containing lyrics to all of the following songs to each group participant. Sing each song as a group and locate each state represented by the following songs on a map. Also have seniors locate the state where they were born to show the group.

- **"Deep in the Heart of Texas"**
- **"The Tennessee Waltz"**
- **"Georgia on My Mind"**
- **"Take Me Home, Country Roads"**

Movement to Music:

Lead a movement to music exercise with the Frank Sinatra recording, **"New York, New York."** Give a variety of movement directions throughout the song. See Part Three for ideas.

Instrumental Performance:

Sing the song, **"This Land is Your Land,"** adding four instrumental parts to represent each of the four United States locations repeated in the chorus; California, New York Island, Redwood Forest, Gulf Stream Waters. Practice playing each instrumental part on cue first, then sing the entire song with all the instrumental parts playing at the appropriate time. See additional resources.

Closing:

Lead the group in singing the song, **"God Bless America,"** 2x.

ADDITIONAL RESOURCES:

"This Land is Your Land" with Instrumental Parts

Start by singing the chorus as a group 2x. Ask seniors to name the four United States locations mentioned in the song—California, New York Island, Redwood Forest, Gulf Stream Waters. Discuss where each place is located in relation to the United States as a whole. California and the Redwood Forest are both on the West Coast of the country, New York and the Gulf Stream are both on the East Coast, so the chorus references the *entire* United States from coast to coast! Divide the group into four sections and assign each section an instrumental part to represent one of the locations in the chorus.

- California: Maracas and/or Shakers
- New York: Jingle Bells
- Redwood Forest: Drums
- Gulf Stream Waters: Hand Bells (notes of the "D" chord)

I like to use cue cards with a picture of each location and assign a group leader to help lead and cue each section. I also like to arrange the sections by location so the group playing the maracas and the group playing the drums are on the therapist's left (West Coast) and the group playing the jingle bells and the group playing the hand bells are on the therapist's right (East Coast), to give the feeling of the sound moving from coast to coast! Each instrumental section plays when their location is sung in the song. Practice each part individually, and then practice all the sections playing on cue while speaking the lyrics. When everyone is comfortable with when to play, sing the entire song though as a group while playing the instruments on cue during the chorus. While some versions of the song go *chorus-verse-verse-verse-chorus*, when performing this way, sing the song, *chorus-verse-chorus-verse-chorus-verse-chorus*, so the instruments can be played as often as possible!

OUTLINE: *Rock & Roll*

Opening:

Lead seniors in singing along with three or four popular/favorite songs.

Introduce Theme:

Introduce the theme of "Rock and Roll" and briefly discuss the history of rock and roll music. Include how it evolved from other musical styles and became so popular. At the time, parents did not like it, but rock and roll is here to stay!

Movement to Music:

Lead a movement to music exercise with two recorded songs, "Little Darlin'" and "Rock and Roll is Here to Stay."

Suggested Movements:

- "Little Darlin'"– Sway side to side, shake and move alternating shoulders, shake shoulders up and down together, roll arms, etc. Focus on upper body/arms.
- "Rock and Roll is Here to Stay"– Tap toes, tap toes side to side (like doing the twist), kicks, dancing/moving feet, etc. Focus on lower body/feet.

Shakeable Instruments:

Pass out a variety of instruments and have seniors shake along with two recorded songs, "Tutti Frutti" and "Good Golly Miss Molly." Briefly model various rhythmic shaking patterns for seniors to follow and then ask each senior to demonstrate a way to shake along for the group to imitate.

Song Packets and Related Exercises:

Pass out song packets containing lyrics to all of the following songs to each group participant. Sing each song as a group and complete related exercises as indicated. See resources as needed.

- "Hound Dog"
- "Earth Angel"
- "Jailhouse Rock"
- "Rockin' Robin"– Have seniors play slide whistles to add fun sound effects.
- "Yakety Yak"– Have seniors sing the repeating line, "Yakety Yak, Don't Talk Back," as a call and a response.
- "Love Me Tender"
- "Johnny B. Goode"

Instrumental Performance:

Pass out a variety of instruments and have seniors shake along and sing the song, "Rock Around the Clock." After the last written verse, modify the song to include directions as to how to play the instruments such as: "We're going to shake up high, shake up high, shake, shake to the sky..." Include directions to play high, low, to the side, fast, slow, loud, and soft.

Closing:

Slow down and lead seniors in a stretching and relaxation exercise with a recording of the song, "In the Still of the Night."

ADDITIONAL RESOURCES:

Origins/History of Rock and Roll
A few brief highlights

- This musical genre developed out of several styles including the blues, gospel music, jazz, and even country western music.
- The earliest forms of rock and roll first appeared in the late 1940s, usually with a piano or saxophone as the lead instrument.
- It first became popular with African Americans after World War II.
- Radio disc jockeys were the first to start calling this new style of music, "rock and roll."
- It initially became popular in small clubs and on the radio. Later, programs such as *American Bandstand* allowed teenagers to watch their favorite bands on television.
- Classic rock and roll (seen around the mid 1950s) generally features one or two electric guitars, a string bass or electric bass guitar, and a drum set.
- The 1950s and 1960s are generally considered the "golden age" of rock and roll.
- The style is characterized by its use of electric guitars and drummers that emphasized the off beats.
- Many parents did not like the loud, fast beat, naughty lyrics, and dancing associated with rock and roll.

"Rockin' Robin" with Slide Whistles
After singing this song through once, introduce the slide whistles and demonstrate how to use the slide to adjust the sound. Pass out slide whistles to each member of the group (or ask for volunteers, depending on the group.) Assist seniors as needed with creating a good sound with the whistles. Encourage everyone to experiment with different sounds. Have seniors imitate bird sounds by moving the slide rapidly while blowing. Instruct seniors to play only during the chorus and practice playing during the chorus once. Perform the entire song as a group 2x with everyone singing the verses and those with slide whistles playing during the chorus.

"Yakety Yak"
At the end of every verse, the line "Yakety yak, Don't talk back," repeats. Have the group sing this part in a call and response style. My seniors like to shout it at each other! Have one side of the room shout "Yakety yak" while the other side answers, "Don't talk back."

OUTLINE: *Hawaiian Luau*

Opening/Introduce Theme:

Lead seniors in singing along with a few popular/favorite songs. Then introduce the theme of "Hawaiian Luau."

Movement to Music:

Lead a movement to music exercise with a recording of the song, **"Little Grass Shack."** Give a variety of movement directions throughout the song. See Part Three for ideas.

Group Discussion:

Lead a discussion about "Hawaii."
For higher functioning seniors, have them close their eyes while you lead a relaxation exercise. Talk them through imagining the sights, sounds, and smells of Hawaii, while softly playing the ocean drum.

Maracas and Shakers:

Pass out maracas and shakers and have seniors shake along with two recorded songs, **"Gay Hawaiian Party"** and **"Hapa Haole Hula Girl."** Direct seniors to shake along in a variety of ways with the rhythm of these songs. See Part Three for ideas. Be sure to include shaking with both arms out to one side and then both arms out to the other side imitating the arms of hula dancers.

Ocean Drum:

Introduce the ocean drum and have seniors listen to the variety of sounds it can make. Prompt seniors to take turns trying it, creating soft and gentle waves, large crashing waves, etc. Ask for volunteers to play it as the session progresses, using it to accompany songs and later playing it in the drum circle.

Song Packets and Related Exercises:

Pass out song packets containing lyrics to all of the following songs to each group participant. Sing each song as a group and complete related exercises as indicated. See resources as needed.

NOTE: *I usually sing some, but not all of these, due to time.*

- **"The *Hukilau* Song"**– Explain the meanings of the Hawaiian words in the song and have seniors practice saying unfamiliar words. Discuss what the song is about before singing it 2x.
- **"A Sleepy Lagoon"**
- **"Beyond the Reef"**
- **"Surfin' Safari"**
- **"Under the Boardwalk"**– Have seniors play a rhythmic, cabasa accompaniment with this song.

Modified Hula Dancing:

Explain that while most people may first think about hip movements in hula dancing, one of the most important parts of hula dancing is actually the arms, as hula dancers use their arms to help tell the story of the song. Teach arm movements to "hula dance" and tell the story of the song, **"Hawaiian Rainbows."** Sing the song through 2x first, then teach arm movements one line at a time. Practice first, and then perform the entire song 2x as a group with the therapist singing and leading on guitar.

Closing:

Pass out drums and a variety of percussion instruments and lead seniors in a drum circle.

ADDITIONAL RESOURCES:

"The Hukilau Song" Lyric Translations

The song was written by Jack Owens in 1948 after attending a luau in Laie, Hawaii.

- *Laulau* is a Hawaiian dish in which pork or fish is cooked in an underground oven, wrapped in leaves and covered by hot rocks.
- *Kaukau* means food or 'to eat'. It is not actually a Hawaiian word.
- A *Luau* is a Hawaiian feast.
- *'Ama'ama* means fish.

Hawaii Group Discussion Prompts

What things come to mind when thinking about Hawaii? What are some things you might do in Hawaii? Has anyone ever been to Hawaii? What sorts of foods come from Hawaii?

Ideas include: Luaus (discuss what sort of things you might eat and do at a luau), hula dancers, leis, grass skirts, ukuleles, the ocean, the beach, palm trees, beautiful weather, tropical flowers, volcanos, pineapples, coconuts, macadamia nuts, fish (specifically Mahi Mahi and Tuna).

NOTE: *For some of my groups of seniors, I like to use pictures of Hawaii and Hawaiian things as a way to prompt them and aid them during group discussions.*

Modified Hula Dancing to "Hawaiian Rainbows"

Hawaiian Rainbows

"Hawaiian Rainbows, white clouds roll by;	Move arms in a large arc resembling a rainbow, then roll arms.
You show your colors, against the sky.	Raise arms from the lap up towards the ceiling.
Hawaiian Rainbows, it seems to me;	Move arms in a large arc resembling a rainbow, then point to yourself.
Reach from the mountains, down to the sea."	Make an "A" with the arms by touching finger tips, then move the arms like a hula dancer, across the body, imitating the ocean's surface.

OUTLINE: *Words of Wisdom*

Opening/Introduce Theme:

Lead seniors in singing along with several popular/favorite songs. Include a few slower songs and plenty of upbeat songs. Then introduce the theme of music that contains advice or words of wisdom.

Movement to Music:

Lead a movement to music exercise with a recording of the song, **"You Can't Hurry Love,"** by the Supremes. Give a variety of movement directions throughout the song. See Part Three for ideas. Ask seniors to identify what advice the song gives (you can't hurry love, love is a lot of give and take). Ask them if they agree with that advice and to share what they have learned about love.

Group Discussion:

Ask seniors to complete common adages. Discuss what each phrase means and if they agree or disagree with the advice given.

Song Packets and Related Exercises:

Pass out song packets containing lyrics to all of the following songs to each group participant. Sing each song as a group and complete related exercises as indicated. See resources as needed.

- **"Accentuate the Positive"** – Have seniors identify and discuss the advice given in the song.
- **"Button Up Your Overcoat"** – Ask each senior to recall at least one piece of advice given in the song.
- **"Que Sera, Sera"** – Ask seniors what sort of advice their parents gave them when they were young. Then ask what sort of advice and words of wisdom they would like to pass on to their children and grandchildren.
- **"Don't Worry, Be Happy"** – Discuss the song and then add drums and hand bells to the accompaniment.

Closing:

Pass out drums and a variety of percussion instruments and lead seniors in a drum circle.

ADDITIONAL RESOURCES:

Common Adages
Ask seniors to complete each one.

The early bird (gets the worm).

You can lead a horse to water (but you can't make him drink).

Never look a gift horse (in the mouth).

A stitch in time (saves nine).

A penny saved (is a penny earned).

The grass is always greener (on the other side).

A bird in the hand (is worth two in the bush).

Don't count your chickens (before they hatch).

Don't put the cart before (the horse).

It's no use crying over (spilled milk).

Birds of a feather (flock together).

Actions speak louder (than words).

Don't judge a book (by its cover).

"Don't Worry, Be Happy"

Sing through the song and then lead a group discussion about the song lyrics. What advice does the song give? Is it good advice? What are common things that people worry about? Discuss the difference between simply *worrying* about things over which you have no control (in which case worry is a negative emotion and un-productive) versus being concerned about problems that are in your control, in which case worry can be positive *if* it leads to taking action.

Add drums and hand bells to help accompany the song and emphasize the advice given. Have some seniors play the drums on the word, "worry," every time it is sung and other seniors play the hand bells (forming the tonic of whatever key in which you are performing the song, I prefer the key of "C") on the word, "happy," every time it is sung. Sing through the song with the instrumental parts added.

OUTLINE: *School Days*

Opening:

Lead seniors in singing along with several popular/favorite songs. Include a few slower songs and plenty of upbeat songs. Include multiple verses of the song, **"When the Saints Go Marching In."**

Drumming:

Pass out drums and a variety of percussion instruments and lead seniors in a drum circle.

Introduce Theme/Group Discussion:

Introduce the theme of "Back to School." Lead the group in a discussion about their school day experiences. Discussion prompts might include: "What was your favorite subject in school?" "What were your favorite things about going back to school in the fall?" "Tell us about a favorite memory from when you were in school!" "What was your school like?" "Did you make any lifelong friends in school?"

Shakeable Instruments:

Pass out a variety of instruments and shake along with two recorded songs, **"Charlie Brown"** and **"School Days"** (by Chuck Berry). Direct seniors to shake along in a variety of ways with the rhythm of these songs. See Part Three for ideas.

Song Packets and Related Exercises:

Pass out song packets containing lyrics to all of the following songs to each group participant. Sing each song as a group and complete related exercises as indicated. See resources as needed.

- **"School Days"**– (The version from 1907 by Will Cobb and Gus Edwards) Sing it 2x.
- **"Hail, Hail, the Gang's All Here"**– Just sing it once first, then add movements with each successive repetition of the song.
- **"The Wiffenpoof Song"**
- **"Getting to Know You"**

Group Songwriting:

Since there are not many songs about going to school, have your seniors write their own! Work as a group to write multiple verses of a song about going to school, favorite school days activities, and favorite memories to the tune of **"When the Saints Go Marching In."**

Closing:

Lead the group in singing the song, **"Farewell Ladies, Farewell Gentlemen."**

ADDITIONAL RESOURCES:

"Hail, Hail the Gang's All Here" Movement to Music

Sing the song through multiple times adding a different movement direction each time. Combine some of the movement directions on top of each other so each repetition requires greater coordination.

Examples:
- Tap Toes
- March
- March and Pat Knees
- March and Clap
- Alternate between Clapping Hands and Patting Knees
- March while Alternating between Clapping Hands and Patting Knees

School Days Songwriting

To the tune of "When the Saints Go Marching In"

I like to write multiple verses by having seniors give two suggestions, singing that verse, asking for two more suggestions, singing it with the new suggestions and so on.

Oh when those school bells, begin to ring,

Oh when those school bells begin to ring,

We just can't wait to _____ and _____,

When those school bells begin to ring!

OUTLINE: *Autumn*

Opening:

Lead seniors in singing along with several popular/favorite songs. Include a few slower songs and plenty of upbeat songs.

Introduce Theme:

Introduce today's theme of autumn. Briefly review last week's discussion of going back to school (if applicable). The start of school signifies the start of fall for many people, even long after they are no longer attending school.

Movement to Music:

Lead a movement to music exercise with a recording of the song, **"September in the Rain."**

Suggested Movements: Tap toes, tap toes side to side (rotating at the ankle), shake shoulders, sway side to side, swing arms side to side, kick with alternating legs.

Group Discussion:

Lead a group discussion about "Autumn." Discussion prompts might include: "What do you think about when you think about the season of autumn?" (school, football season, cooler weather, changing leaves, falling leaves, shorter days, Halloween, Thanksgiving, migrating birds, etc.) "What are your favorite things about autumn?" "What are some foods we eat in autumn?" (chili, pumpkin pie, apples, pecan pie, apple cider, etc.)

Instrumental Performance:

Sing the song, **"Don't Sit Under the Apple Tree,"** once as a group. Then add instrumental parts to accent each line. Practice each instrumental part alone with the words so they know when to start and stop. Then sing the song through as a group 2x with the added instrumental parts. See additional resources.

Song Packets and Related Exercises:

Pass out song packets containing lyrics to all of the following songs to each group participant. Sing each song as a group and complete related exercises as indicated. See resources as needed.

- **"Autumn Leaves"**– Sing 2x.
- **"Everything is Beautiful"**
- **"Shine On, Harvest Moon"**– Sing 3x.

Group Songwriting:

Since there are not many songs about autumn, have your seniors write their own! Work as a group to write multiple verses of a song about autumn to the tune of **"She'll be Coming 'Round the Mountain."**

Closing:

Lead a relaxation and stretching exercise with a recording of the song, **"Autumn in New York."** I prefer the Jo Stafford version.

ADDITIONAL RESOURCES:

Autumn Songwriting
To the tune of "She'll Be Coming 'Round the Mountain"
There are two possible ways to do this:

1 Write multiple verses by having seniors give only two suggestions at a time so essentially the song is one line that repeats 5x, like the original version of "She'll Be Coming 'Round the Mountain." Then sing another verse with two different suggestions repeating the same two ideas throughout the song and so on.

Oh we think of _____(X)_____ and _____(Y)_____ when Autumn comes,

Oh we think of _____(X)_____ and _____(Y)_____ when Autumn comes,

Oh we think of _____(X)_____ and _____(Y)_____ , yes we think of _____(X)_____ and _____(Y)_____ ,

Oh we think of _____(X)_____ and _____(Y)_____ when Autumn comes!

2 Write out the song as below and fill in different ideas in each blank, so there is no repetition but different ideas with each line.

Oh we think of _____(A)_____ and _____(B)_____ when Autumn comes,

Oh we think of _____(C)_____ and _____(D)_____ when Autumn comes,

Oh we think of _____(E)_____ and _____(F)_____ , yes we think of Fall's best things,

Oh we think of _____(G)_____ and _____(H)_____ when Autumn comes!

"Don't Sit Under the Apple Tree"
Instruct seniors to play the following suggested instrumental parts to highlight each line as indicated, each time the line is repeated throughout the course of the song.

- "Don't sit...apple tree," ~ Drums
- "Don't go...lovers' lane," ~ Drums
- "with anyone else," ~ Maracas
- "but me," ~ Jingle Bells
- "'til...marching home," ~ All Instrumental Parts

"Autumn in New York" Suggested Movements
Complete each of the following movements a few times. Start with a few deep breaths, raise and lower shoulders slowly, roll shoulders slowly, tilt head to shoulder on right, tilt head to shoulder on the left, stretch arms up to the sky, then out to the sides and down. Stretch arms out to the front and push to the sides like swimming, roll ankles one at a time, point foot towards the floor and then flex back towards yourself and then alternate feet, etc.

OUTLINE: *1940s*

NOTE: *This session contains a large amount of material. Depending on the size and the ability level of the group, you may not be able to get through all of it and should edit it for time accordingly.*

Opening/Introduce Theme:

Introduce the theme of the 1940s. Discuss products and famous people of the 1940s. Have seniors share what they remember about the 1940s.

Shakeable Instruments:

Pass out a variety of instruments and shake along with two recorded songs, **"Rum and Coca-Cola,"** and **"Chattanooga Shoe Shine Boy."** Direct seniors to shake along in various ways with the rhythm of these songs. See Part Three for ideas.

Drums and Maracas:

Introduce the song, **"This Land Is Your Land,"** composed by Woodie Guthrie in 1942 and now one of our most well known folk songs. Pass out drums to one side of the group and maracas to the other side. Have the seniors with the drums beat a steady accompaniment on the chorus and the seniors with the maracas shake along on the verses. Sing the song together as a group while adding this musical accompaniment.

Movement to Music:

Lead a movement to music exercise with a recording of the song, **"String of Pearls,"** or **"I've Got a Gal in Kalamazoo."** Give a variety of movement directions throughout the song. See Part Three for ideas.

Song Packets and Event Timeline:

Pass out song packets containing lyrics to all of the following songs to each group participant.

Sing each song as a group and discuss an event from each year of the 1940s. Have an event from each year on a card with a picture and/or description to aid in the group discussion. Have seniors take turns reading a card to the group before placing it in the appropriate place on a 1940s timeline.

- 1940 "You Are My Sunshine"
- 1941 "Don't Sit Under the Apple Tree"– Sing 2x, tap toes first time through, clap along second time through
- 1942 "Deep in the Heart of Texas"
- 1943 "Oh, What A Beautiful Morning"
- 1944 "I'll Be Seeing You"
- 1945 "Sentimental Journey"– Add rhythmic cabasa accompaniment.
- 1946 "Zip-A-Dee-Doo-Dah"
- 1947 "Buttons and Bows"
- 1948 "I'm Looking Over a Four Leaf Clover"
- 1949 "Some Enchanted Evening"

Closing:

Have seniors play maracas, shakers, and cabasas along with a recording of the song, **"Ghost Riders in the Sky,"** from 1948. For more advanced groups, have seniors with cabasas play only during the verses and the seniors with maracas and/or shakers play only during the chorus.

ADDITIONAL RESOURCES:

 Famous Faces of the 1940s
Possibly use pictures to aid in the group discussion.

Gene Kelly	Jimmy Stewart
Hank Williams	Jackie Robinson
Ella Fitzgerald	John Wayne
Bing Crosby	Glenn Miller
Walt Disney	Sugar Ray Robinson
Louis Armstrong	Joe DiMaggio
Vivien Leigh	Rita Hayworth
Cary Grant	Bob Hope
Judy Garland	Frank Sinatra
Duke Ellington	Abbott and Costello

 Famous Products of the 1940s
Possibly use pictures to aid with group discussions.

M & Ms	Slinky
Bikinis	Silly Putty
Bug Spray	Aluminum Foil
Chiquita Bananas	Jeeps
Tupperware	Cake Mix
Television	

Events of the 1940s

For use with the 1940s song packets and timeline

1940 McDonald's Restaurant is founded

1941 Japan bombs Pearl Harbor and the United States enters World War II

1942 The movie *Casablanca* opens

1943 The musical *Oklahoma!* opens on Broadway

1944 The Battle of Normandy begins on June 6th, also known as D-Day

1945 Wold War II Ends; Victory in Europe ~ May 7-8th, Victory in Japan~ August 15th

1946 Tupperware first appears in stores

1947 The Dead Sea Scrolls are first discovered

1948 Warner Brothers shows its first color newsreel

1949 The first Polaroid camera is sold for $89.95

OUTLINE: *Camping*

Opening:

Pass out drums and a variety of percussion instruments and lead seniors in a drum circle.

Introduce Theme/Group Discussion:

Introduce the theme of "Camping" and discuss. Discussion prompts might include: "What things do you need on a camping trip?" "Has anyone in this group been camping and have favorite camping memories?" "Where are some good places to go camping?" "What sort of things do you do on a camping trip?" Use this discussion to lead into a "campfire" sing-along, using song packets full of classic campfire sing-a-long songs!

Song Packets and Related Exercises:

Pass out song packets containing lyrics to all of the following songs to each group participant. Sing each song as a group and complete related exercises as indicated. See resources as needed.

NOTE: *I usually sing some, but not all of these, due to time.*

- "By the Light of the Silvery Moon"
- "Buffalo Gals"
- "She'll Be Coming 'Round the Mountain"
- "Clementine"
- "Home on the Range"

- "Camptown Races"– Sing the 'doo-dah' part in a call and response style, the therapist sings first and the group echoes back; encourage loud and enthusiastic participation! Practice the call and response part first, then sing the entire song.
- "Take Me Home, Country Roads"

Musical Story-Writing:

Have seniors complete a fill-in-the-blank style ghost story.

After the seniors have completed writing the story, ask for volunteers to add musical sound effects for each line. Have each volunteer choose an instrument to represent his or her line. Practice the story with each volunteer, adding his or her sound effect at the appropriate time. Have seniors play louder and faster when the story says "louder" and "faster." Then give a dramatic telling of the story including the musical sound effects. I try to bring as many and as varied instruments as I can and this is a great time to incorporate all of those fun, less-traditional instruments in your collection. Seniors always love trying something new!

Closing:

Lead the group in singing the song, **"Happy Trails."**

ADDITIONAL RESOURCES:

Camping Supplies and Activities

For use in the group discussion:

Sleeping Bag	Fishing
Tent	Hiking
Campfire	Swimming
Firewood	Relaxing in Nature
Flashlight	Ghost Stories
S'mores	Campfire Sing- Along
Roast Hot Dogs	

NOTE: For some of my groups, I like to use pictures as a prompt and aid in group discussions.

A Sample Fill-in-the-Blank Ghost Story

It was a dark and stormy night.

The wind was howling through the trees.

In the air there was a feeling of _____.

Suddenly, we heard a _____.

We looked but only saw _____.

Then we heard the sound of _____.

The sounds grew louder and louder and louder!

Suddenly there appeared _____.

It started to _____.

So we turned and ran faster and faster and faster!

OUTLINE: *Broadway* I

Opening:

Lead seniors in singing along with several popular/favorite songs.

Introduce Theme/Group Discussion:

Introduce the theme of "Broadway Musicals." Discuss the history of Broadway and ask seniors about what Broadway Musicals they have seen.

Movement to Music:

Lead a movement to music exercise with a recording of the song, **"Hello, Dolly!"** from the musical, *Hello, Dolly!*

Suggested Movements: Tap toes side to side (twisting at the ankle), extend leg forward and tap heel (alternate legs), move one foot out to the side and then back in towards center (alternate feet), chorus-line kicks (alternate legs), shake and move shoulders.

Movement to Music:

Teach a choreographed dance to the song, **"A Bushel and a Peck,"** from the musical, *Guys and Dolls*. Practice the movements and then have the group verbally review the order of the movements several times. Play the recording and dance along!

Song Packets and Related Exercises:

Pass out song packets containing lyrics to all of the following songs to each group participant. Sing each song as a group.

- **"Give My Regards to Broadway"**
- **"The Lullaby of Broadway"**
- **"There's No Business Like Show Business"**
- **"I've Got Rhythm"**
- **"Alexander's Ragtime Band"**

Maracas and Shakers:

Pass out maracas and shakers to shake along with a recording of the song, **"I'm Gonna Wash That Man Right Outa My Hair,"** from the musical, *South Pacific*. Shake side to side as if doing the twist with the rhythm of the song. Shake while moving arms in a big circle during the slower sections.

Kazoos:

Introduce the song, **"The Lonely Goatherd,"** from the musical, *The Sound of Music*. Explain that the song requires some yodeling and ask if anyone in the group can yodel. Introduce the kazoo as an instrument to help with the yodeling sound effects of the song. Play a recording of the song and lead the group in playing the kazoos each time yodeling occurs in the song.

Play a recording of the song, **"Yankee Doodle Dandy,"** from the 1904 musical, *Little Johnny Jones*. Lead seniors in playing their kazoos along with the melody of this song.

Closing:

Lead the group in playing the song, **"Farewell Ladies, Farewell Gentlemen,"** on their kazoos.

ADDITIONAL RESOURCES:

Broadway Musicals Discussion Prompts

Where is Broadway? (New York City) What is a Musical? (It is like a play, but with lots of music, singing, and dancing woven into the story.) Has anyone here ever seen a musical? What did you see? Did you enjoy the show? Where did you see it? You do not have to go to New York to see a Broadway Musical, many productions travel around the country! You can also sometimes see musicals on TV. **History of Broadway:** In 1750, the first theater company opened on Nassau Street. Soon a second theater was built. However, most productions were Shakespeare plays or ballad operas. In the 1800's several more theaters were built and minstrel shows, variety shows, and operas were popular. Musicals were first performed during this time and theater moved to Broadway street due to inexpensive real estate prices. Broadway entered its "golden age" after the Great Depression and at this point, musicals became productions with the music and storyline completely integrated.

"A Bushel and a Peck" Choreographed Dance

The Doris Day Version of the Song

For each verse, repeat the following sequence of movements:

- Instrumental Introduction ~ Shake Shoulders
- First Part of the Verse ("I love you a bushel and a peck...") ~ A Movement with the Feet
- Second Part of the Verse ("About you....") ~ Sway Side to Side
- The "A-doodle-oodle-ooh-doo" Part ~ Roll Arms

Use a different foot movement with each verse including: Tap Toes, Extend Leg Forward and Tap Heel (Alternating Legs), Kick with Alternating Legs, Move Feet Out to the Side and Back to Center with Alternating Feet

 ### Introducing and Using the Kazoo

Explain and demonstrate that the kazoo cannot be played by just blowing into it like a whistle, but should be played by humming or making an "oooh" sound into the large end. Pass out kazoos to each member of the group. Provide additional assistance with playing the kazoo to each group member as needed. Many of the seniors in my groups initially had trouble, but with a little extra assistance were able to play with ease. I buy cheap kazoos in bulk when we use them in a group (which is rarely) and let each senior keep their kazoo after the session. Kazoos are not really built to last and are too difficult to sanitize effectively.

OUTLINE: *Broadway* II

Opening:

Lead seniors in singing along with several popular/favorite songs. Sing the chorus of the song, **"Give My Regards to Broadway,"** 2x as well.

Introduce Theme:

Introduce today's theme of "Broadway Musicals" as a continuation of the previous session. Briefly review the discussion of Broadway from the last session and mention how many great Broadway songs have become even more famous and well-loved than the musicals they were in originally.

NOTE: *Throughout the duration of the session, ask the group if they can name which Broadway Musical originally featured each song presented. Then briefly review its plot.*

Song Packets and Related Exercises:

Pass out song packets containing lyrics to all of the following songs to each group participant. Sing each song as a group and complete related exercises as indicated. See resources as needed.

- **"Oklahoma!"** (From *Oklahoma!*)– Encourage seniors to enthusiastically shout the "Oklahomas" and other exclamations in the song as they sing.
- **"Some Enchanted Evening"** (From *South Pacific*)
- **"Getting to Know You"** (From *The King and I*)
- **"I Could Have Danced All Night"** (From *My Fair Lady*)
- **"Edelweiss"** (From *The Sound of Music*)
- **"Consider Yourself"** (From *Oliver!*)

Bells and Tambourines:

Pass out bells and tambourines to shake along with a recording of the song, **"I Feel Pretty,"** from the musical, *West Side Story*. Sway side to side with the rhythm of the song while playing along.

NOTE: *Use a version that does not contain the interjections originally a part of the song in the musical for ease and flow when playing along.*

Shakeable Instruments:

Pass out a variety of instruments and have seniors shake along with a recording of the song, **"Anything You Can Do,"** from the musical, *Annie Get Your Gun*. Direct seniors to shake along in a variety of ways with the rhythm of the song, being prepared for the tempo and rhythm changes that occur.

Boomwhackers:

Pass out Boomwhackers and have seniors play a steady beat with a recording of the song, **"Seventy-Six Trombones,"** from the musical, *The Music Man*. The song is in 6/8 time. With each verse, alternate between playing only on beat 1 and playing on beats 1 and 4.

Closing:

Slow down and lead seniors in a stretching and relaxation exercise with a recording of the song, **"Sunrise, Sunset,"** from the musical, *Fiddler on the Roof*.

ADDITIONAL RESOURCES:

Brief Musical Summaries

Oklahoma! (1943) ~ The first musical written by the team of Rodgers and Hammerstein, this story is set in Oklahoma territory in 1906. The plot revolves around the love story of a cowboy, Curly, and a farm girl, Laurey. The musical also addresses class issues between farmers and cowboys in the American West, as Oklahoma becomes established as a state.

Annie Get Your Gun (1946) ~ This musical tells the (fictionalized) love story of Annie Oakley and Frank Butler, both amazing sharpshooters in Buffalo Bill's Wild West Show.

South Pacific (1949) ~ This musical was also written by the team of Rodgers and Hammerstein and is set on a South Pacific island during World War II. It follows two troubled love stories; one between a young nurse, Nellie, and a middle-aged French plantation owner, Emile de Beque, and another between U.S. Lieutenant Cable and a young Tonkinese woman, Liat. Issues of racial prejudice are also addressed.

The King and I (1951) ~ The fifth musical written by the team of Rodgers and Hammerstein is set in Thailand in the 1860s. The King hires a British governess, Anna, for his children, in hopes that she can help his family to understand and adopt western customs, as his country is becoming more westernized. Anna and the King initially are at odds, but later fall in love, which neither can fully admit or express.

My Fair Lady (1956) ~ This musical is based on the play, *Pygmalion*, by George Bernard Shaw. It tells the story of professor Higgins and his attempt to turn cockney girl, Eliza, into a proper-speaking lady. His tutoring is a success and Eliza passes for a princess at a ball. Though initially Higgins treats Eliza with little respect and as a mere experiment, he eventually falls in love with her.

West Side Story (1957) ~ Set in New York City, this musical tells the ill-fated love story of Maria and Tony, who are a part of rival gangs, the Puerto Rican Sharks and the American Jets.

The Music Man (1957) ~ This musical tells the story of con man Harold Hill, who attempts to make his fortune selling instruments to the town of River City, Iowa to start a band he never intends to lead. However, he ends up falling in love with Marian, the librarian and piano teacher, and becomes an honest man.

The Sound of Music (1959) ~ This musical tells the story of Maria, a soon to be nun, who is sent off to be a governess for Captain von Trapp's seven children. Maria and the children bond over a love of music. Eventually the widowed Captain and Maria fall in love and are married, but the entire family is forced to flee when the Nazi's invade.

Oliver! (1963) ~ Based on the Dickens novel, *Oliver Twist*, this musical tells the story of a young orphan boy's struggles to survive in London. After a series of bad situations including a workhouse and working for a violent thief, Oliver eventually finds his great uncle and the home he always wanted.

Fiddler on the Roof (1964) ~ This musical tells the story of Tevye, a Jewish dairyman, and his wife and three daughters, living a life full of Jewish traditions in Russia amid growing hostilities. Rather than following along with the matchmaker and their father's wishes, one by one, each of the three girls find a husband and marry for love, Unfortunately, the family is eventually forced to leave their homes.

OUTLINE: *Texas*

NOTE: *This session is a huge hit in my home state of Texas. I wanted to include it even for those not working in this state in hopes that it would give you ideas for building a similar hometown pride/state pride session for your seniors!*

Opening/Introduce Theme:

Pass out a variety of small percussion instruments and lead seniors in singing and shaking along with a few popular/favorite songs. Then introduce the theme of "Texas."

Movement to Music:

Lead a movement to music exercise with a recording of the song, **"San Antonio Stroll."**

Suggested Movements: Tap toes, tap heels, march in place, pat knees, clap hands, alternate between patting knees and clapping (pat-clap-pat-clap), etc.

Group Discussion:

Lead a discussion about "Texas." Discussion prompts could include: "Who here in the group was born in Texas?" or "What are your favorite things about living in Texas?" and "What are some famous cities in Texas?" and "What are some of its historical sites, native plants, and animals?" etc.

Instrumental Performance:

Sing **"Deep in the Heart of Texas"** and discuss what attributes of Texas are listed in the song. Use a different instrument to create sound effects for each different line describing Texas. Ask for a volunteer to 'solo' on each line and allow them to choose an instrument to play to represent their line. Practice following cues to start and stop playing.

Then sing the entire song 2x as a group with the different instrumental sound effects throughout. Cues cards with pictures for each line provide helpful reminders as well.

Hand Bells:

Sing the song, **"The Yellow Rose of Texas,"** 2x. Then use hand bells to create an accompaniment. Ask for volunteers to each play a hand bell and create two groups. One group plays the bells to form an "E" chord, the other group plays the bells to form a "B7" chord. Have seniors practice playing the bells on cue, then have the whole group sing while the volunteers provide the accompaniment with the hand bells as cued by the therapist.

Drumming:

Pass out drums and lead seniors in playing together on a steady beat. Keep this steady beat going as the group sings the song, **"The Eyes of Texas."** Then change the drum pattern to a long-short-long (think dotted quarter note, eighth note, dotted quarter etc.) and have seniors drum the new pattern while singing the song 2x. Lead into a drum circle if there is time.

Closing:

Pass out additional drums and percussion instruments as needed and lead seniors in a drum circle, if there is time. If out of time, lead the group in singing the song, **"Happy Trails."**

ADDITIONAL RESOURCES:

"Our State/City" Additional Resources

Some ideas to get you started planning a session for the seniors in your area!

All about Our State/City Discussion Prompts

Some Points to Consider:

- Weather/Climate
- Terrain
- Native/Common Plants
- Animals
- Local Foods
- Landmarks
- Historical Significance
- Famous People
- Traditions/Culture
- What makes this place special?

Possible Musical Selections To Use

- Songs about our state or city
- Song styles prevalent for that area (i.e. Country-Western music for the city of Nashville or the state of Tennessee; Broadway musicals for New York; Jazz for New Orleans/Louisiana, etc.)
- Famous singers/song writers from that area (i.e Elvis songs for Memphis/Tennessee; Stephen Foster folk songs for Pittsburgh/Pennsylvania; Bing Crosby for Washington State; Frank Sinatra for New Jersey, Dinah Washington for Chicago, etc.)

OUTLINE: *Let's Dance*

Opening/Introduce Theme:

Lead seniors in singing along with several popular/favorite songs. Include **"I've Been Working on the Railroad"** adding directions for seniors to tap toes, march, and/or clap along with the beat. Then introduce the theme of "Dancing."

Movement to Music:

Lead a movement to music exercise with a recording of the song, **"You Make Me Want to Shout."** Teach and practice choreographed dance moves first, then put on the music and perform the dance together as a group!

Shakeable Instruments:

Pass out a variety of instruments and shake along with the following recorded songs.

- **"The Twist"** – Have seniors shake side to side while twisting (seated) with the beat.
- **"Shake, Rattle, and Roll"** – Have seniors shake high and then low, shake forward and then back, shake out to opposite sides and then back in to the center, shake while moving arms in a circular motion, and then shake as fast as they can like a "rumble."

Song Packets and Related Exercises:

Pass out song packets containing lyrics to all of the following songs to each group participant. Sing each song as a group and complete related exercises as indicated. See resources as needed.

- **"I Could Have Danced All Night"** – Lead a discussion about dancing.
- **"The Tennessee Waltz"** – Have seniors sway side to side with the rhythm of this song.

- **"Music, Music, Music"**
- **"I've Got Rhythm"**
- **"Twist and Shout"** – Practice the text first, then sing in a call and response style.

Modified Hokey Pokey:

Lead seniors in singing and dancing (seated) along with the song, **"The Hokey Pokey."** Lead on guitar and model movements as much as possible with each verse. Have seniors take turns suggesting which movements should come next and then perform it as a group. Body parts to "put in" might include the following, all of which work just fine from a seated position:

Right Foot, Left Foot, Both Feet, Right Arm/Hand, Left Arm/Hand, Both Arms/Hands, Right Elbow, Left Elbow, Head, Right Shoulder, Left Shoulder, Right Knee, Left Knee, Whole self ~ Have seniors bend forward at the waist and back if seated

Closing:

Lead seniors in a movement to music exercise with the Frank Sinatra recording, **"Let's Face the Music and Dance."**

ADDITIONAL RESOURCES:

"You Make Me Want to Shout" Choreographed Dance

First, practice with seniors instructing them put their arms up and yell "shout" every time they hear it in the song. Also review other movements used in the song before putting on the recording and dancing.

Beginning of the song until the verse "I still remember" starts	Raise arms and shout with the rhythm of the song, on the words, "shout" and "say"
From the line "I still remember" until the line "I want you to know" (when the song slows)	Shake and move shoulders
During the slower section until the chorus, "Shout," starts again	Tap toes with the beat
From the chorus of repeated "Shouts" until the song really slows down.	Raise arms and shout with the rhythm of the song on the word "shout"
During the very slow section	Take two deep breaths, and then slowly roll shoulders
During the chorus of repeated "shouts" (getting softer and then louder) through the end of the song.	Raise arms and shout with the rhythm of the song on the word "shout." Then roll arms as the song gets softer and then louder. Make smaller and smaller circles as the song gets softer and softer and larger and larger circles as the song gets louder and louder. Then return to raising arms and shouting with the rhythm of the song on the word "shout."

"Dancing" Discussion Prompts

Ask seniors if they liked to go dancing. What styles of dance do (did) they enjoy the most? Who did they go dancing with? Where did they like to go dancing? See how many styles of dancing they can name such as ballet, slow dancing, country line dancing, square dancing, polka dancing, swing dancing, the jitterbug, the tango, the Charleston, the Waltz, etc.

"Twist and Shout"

This song can be challenging for some seniors, but a lot of fun. Before singing the song, practice speaking the text (rhythmically) in a call and response style with the group. The therapist says a line and then the group repeats. In the original version, the first line is often longer than the repeated line. However, it is much easier for most seniors if you modify the song so that the "call" line and the "response" line are the same. This works just as well as the original lyrics.

Ex. Instead of "C'mon c'mon, c'mon, c'mon, baby, now (Come on baby)," just sing "C'mon, baby, now (Come on baby)."

OUTLINE: *Love & Marriage*

Opening/Introduce Theme:

Lead a stretching exercise to a recording of "**Ave Maria**" by Schubert. Then introduce the theme of "Love & Marriage." Possibly sing a few traditional love songs (i.e. "**Let Me Call You Sweetheart**," "**Yes Sir! That's My Baby**," etc.)

Shakeable Instruments:

Pass out a variety of instruments and shake along with two recorded songs, "**Get Me to the Church on Time**" and "**Not Too Young, Not to Get Married.**" Direct seniors to shake along in various ways with the rhythm of these songs. See Part Three for ideas.

Music Listening/Reminiscence:

Play a recording of the song, "**Here Comes the Bride**," and ask seniors to identify the tune. Listen for a little while and as the song finishes playing in the background, ask seniors to name what sort of things they think about when they think about weddings. For example, cake, bride and groom, church, decorations, friends and family, flowers, white dress and veil, champagne, etc.

Play a recording of Pachelbel's "**Canon in D**" and ask seniors to close their eyes and think back to their wedding day. Depending on the group, do a guided reminiscence exercise. Ask each senior to share about what made his or her wedding day special.

Song Packets and Related Exercises:

Pass out song packets containing lyrics to all of the following songs to each group participant. Sing each song as a group and complete related exercises as indicated. See resources as needed.

- "**Always**"
- "**Love Me Tender**"
- "**I Could Have Danced All Night**"
- "**I'm In the Mood For Love**"
- "**What a Wonderful World**"
- "**Bicycle Built for Two**"– Sing the song (both verses) once, and then sing it again in call and response style. One section takes Harry's part, the next section takes Daisy's response. You could divide guys and girls or one side of the group and the other, depending on group demographics. Then discuss: Do you agree or disagree with Daisy's response and why?
- "**Fly Me to the Moon**"

Movement to Music:

Teach a choreographed dance to the song, "**Going to the Chapel.**" Practice the movements for each part first and then play the recording and dance along!

Closing:

Have seniors drum along with a recording of Mendelssohn's "**Wedding March.**" Start with drum rolls and then play with a steady beat, following the rhythm of the music.

ADDITIONAL RESOURCES:

"Ave Maria" Suggested Stretching Ideas

Start with a deep breath. Stretch arms up to the ceiling and slowly lower down to the sides (2x). Stretch arms out to the front and push out to the sides like swimming and down (2x). Slowly raise and lower shoulders (2x). Do slow shoulder rolls, a few times rolling in each direction. Lightly roll head/feel head floating on top of the body. Stretch right leg out in front and point and flex toes (slowly 2x). Stretch left leg out in front and point and flex toes (slowly 2x). Stretch out each foot and roll ankles one at a time. Finish with a deep breath.

Wedding Day Reminiscence, Guided Recall

Start by picturing the person you are about to marry. What is he/she wearing? How do you feel when you look at him/her? Think about all the times you have shared leading up to this day! What are you wearing? What sort of preparations did you make before the ceremony? Now picture where you both are getting married. Is it a church, a courthouse, a home? Look around the room, remembering the decorations-flowers, maybe candles. Who is there at the ceremony with you? Friends? Family? After the ceremony what are you going to do to celebrate? Is there a cake and punch? Maybe a dinner? Dancing and champagne? As you think about your wedding day, what made it special? What was your favorite part of the day? Now slowly take a deep breath and open your eyes.

"Going to the Chapel" Choreographed Dance

Chorus: Claps to the side—to the right 8x, to the left 8x, to the right 8x, to the left 8x

Verse 1: Heel taps—extend leg forward and tap heel, use alternating feet

Verse 2: Big sway side to side

OUTLINE: *Happiness*

Opening/Introduce Theme:

Pass out drums and a variety of percussion instruments and lead seniors in a drum circle. Then introduce the theme of "Happiness."

Song Packets and Related Exercises:

Pass out song packets containing lyrics to all of the following songs to each group participant. Sing each song as a group and complete related exercises as indicated. See resources as needed.

- "Accentuate the Positive"
- "Smiles"
- "Happy Days"
- "My Favorite Things"– Have seniors name and discuss their favorite things.
- "Happy Trails"
- "Don't Worry, Be Happy"

Instrumental Performance and Group Songwriting:

Sing the song, "Don't Worry, Be Happy," together as a group. Then add drums and hand bells to the song to emphasize the emotions, "worry" and "happy." Have some seniors play the drums on the word "worry" and other seniors play the hand bells on the word "happy." Sing through the song with the instrumental parts adding to the accompaniment.

After singing the song through with the addition of the instrumental parts, complete a songwriting exercise having seniors include other positive and negative emotions.

Singing ~ "If You're Happy and You Know It":

Sing the song, "If You're Happy and You Know It," together as a group. Then have seniors change the verses to add a variety of emotions and correlated actions. Also have seniors list and/or discuss things or situations that can cause them to experience that emotion.

NOTE: *I am very cautious about using this intervention as it may seem childish for some seniors. However, others have a lot of fun with it and it works nicely with their other goal areas.*

Movement to Music:

Lead a movement to music exercise with a recording of the song, "Get Happy" by Frank Sinatra or "The Happy Wanderer" by Frank Weir, if there is time. I sometimes prefer to spend more time drumming at the start of the session instead. Give a variety of movement directions throughout the song. See Part Three for ideas.

Closing:

Lead a relaxation exercise using recorded music by **Enya**. Lead seniors in either a series of stretches and deep breathing or have seniors close their eyes and lead them though some guided relaxation, thinking of and imagining a favorite place.

ADDITIONAL RESOURCES:

"Don't Worry, Be Happy" Songwriting

Using only the first verse of the song, "Don't Worry, Be Happy," complete a fill-in-the-blank style songwriting exercise exploring other positive and negative emotions. Replace the word, "worry," with other negative emotions and replace the word, "happy," with other positive emotions. Create and sing multiple versions of the song, encouraging different seniors to make a suggestion each time. Have seniors keep playing the drums on the negative emotions, and the hand bells on the positive emotions. Possibly have them trade instruments so everyone gets to play on both parts.

ex. Don't complain, Be content

Don't be cranky, Be peaceful

Don't get mad, Be calm

Don't whine, Be thankful

Don't get frustrated, Stay relaxed

"If You're Happy and You Know It"

Possible emotions and related actions.

- Angry ~ Shout "I feel mad!"
- Frustrated ~ Stomp your feet
- Tired ~ Stretch and yawn
- Surprised ~ Say, "Oh my!"
- Calm ~ Say, "Ahhhhhh"
- Lonely ~ Call a friend
- Achy ~ Stretch and flex

OUTLINE: *Halloween*

Opening:

Pass out maracas, jingle bells, shakers, and tambourines. Be sure to give each senior a choice.

Have seniors sing and shake along with several upbeat popular/favorite songs including: **"Don't Sit Under the Apple Tree," "Shine on, Harvest Moon,"** and **"Jingle Jangle Jingle."**

Introduce Theme/Group Discussion:

Introduce today's theme of "Halloween." Have seniors discuss "Halloween" including ways to celebrate, things that come to mind when thinking about Halloween, favorite costumes as children, etc. Use pictures for prompts as needed with seniors with dementia or other cognitive difficulties.

Movement to Music:

Teach a choreographed dance to the song, **"The Monster Mash."** Practice the movements for each part first and then play the recording and dance along!

Song Packets and Related Exercises:

Pass out song packets containing lyrics to all of the following songs to each group participant. Sing each song as a group and complete related exercises as indicated. See resources as needed.

- **"Buffalo Gals"**– It's fast and fun, so sing it 2x.
- **"The Witch Doctor"**– Teach the chorus first, by speaking it, and then by having seniors repeat it one line at a time to practice articulation before singing the entire song. At the end of the song, sing the chorus again going faster and faster and faster!
- **"Purple People Eater"**– Teach the chorus and practice articulation (same as above) before singing.

Boomwhackers:

Introduce the boomwhackers and play along with two recorded songs.

"The Munsters" Theme – Put on a recording of the "Munsters" theme song and have seniors play along. Give verbal/modeling prompts to play boomwhackers together, up high, on the floor, on a chair, with a friend, etc. throughout the song.

"The Addams Family" Theme – Sing the melody of the chorus and have seniors practice playing the boomwhackers in place of the finger snaps in the song. Practice the chorus, reminding them to wait on the third line for the two hits. Practice keeping a steady beat during the verses. Once seniors seem comfortable with this pattern, put on the recording and play along, keeping a steady beat on the verses and playing where the finger snaps occur in the chorus.

Closing:

Lead a movement to music exercise with the Frank Sinatra recording, **"Witchcraft."** Give a variety of movement directions throughout the song. See Part Three for ideas.

ADDITIONAL RESOURCES:

"The Monster Mash" Dance

During the introductory verse, make scary monster faces and gestures.

Chorus: *Make monster claws with the hands and swing hands to the right 4x, then to the left 4x and then to the right 4x, then to the left 4x.*

Verses: *On the 1st verse tap toes with the beat*

On the 2nd verse do the twist (while seated)

On the 3rd verse tap toes with the beat

On the 4th verse do the twist (while seated)

 Ideas on How to Introduce the Boomwhackers

Demonstrate how shorter boomwhackers sound higher and longer boomwhackers sound lower. Explain how each different color represents a unique pitch. Also demonstrate how boomwhackers can be played on almost any surface including other boomwhackers, the floor, chairs, wheelchairs, etc., but not your neighbor!! Pass out boomwhackers in sets of two to each senior for them to try, and encourage them to experiment with different ways to play. Then give directions to play high in the air, low/on the floor, play boomwhackers together, play them on their chair/wheelchair, then find a friend seated nearby and play on each other's boomwhackers, etc.

OUTLINE: *Music*

NOTE: *I think this session could be easily split into two different sessions; one containing the material on different songs about music and musical instruments and one all about musical genres, adding in a drum circle for the last 15-20 minutes of each session. However, for many of my groups I prefer to do it as one session and then pick and choose the material that best suits each group's needs.*

Opening/Introduce Theme:

Start with one popular/favorite song to warm up. Then introduce the theme of "Music" and pass out song packets.

Song Packets and Related Exercises ~ The Love of Music:

Pass out song packets containing lyrics to all of the following songs to each group participant. Sing each song as a group and complete related exercises as indicated. See resources as needed.

- "I've Got Rhythm"
- "Music, Music, Music"
- "Do-Re-Mi"– Sing through once, and then add hand bells.

Name that Musical Instrument:

Have seniors work together to name as many different instruments as they can. Then listen to samples of different instruments playing and have them identify what instrument they are hearing. Samples that consist of only one instrument performing work best. Use a poster with different pictures of instruments to narrow their choices.

Group Discussion:

Have seniors name as many different musical styles or genres as they can. Discuss how songs can often be considered more than one style or genre.

Song Packets and Related Exercises ~ Musical Genres:

Pass out song packets containing lyrics to all of the following songs to each group participant. Sing each song as a group and then ask seniors to identify the musical genre.

NOTE: *I usually sing some, but not all of these, due to time.*

- "Jailhouse Rock" (Rock and Roll)
- "This Land" (Folk)
- "Earth Angel" (Doo Wop)
- "Hey, Good Lookin'" (Country)
- "My Girl" (Motown)
- "I Saw the Light" (Gospel)

Music Listening:

Mix recorded tracks representing different musical genres along with the song selections from above. Have seniors listen to examples of different pieces and name the genre or musical style. Lead a movement to music exercise with some of the recorded samples as well.

Closing:

Play a recording of "Largo" from "Winter," from Vivaldi's Four Seasons. After seniors have identified the musical genre, lead them in a stretching/relaxation exercise.

ADDITIONAL RESOURCES:

"Do-Re-Mi" with the Hand Bells

This song involves more hand bell parts than songs in which hand bells are used to create chords, but it is a huge hit with seniors. Use a single hand bell for each note of the scale. Most sets on the market will work best with the song in the key of "C." So the syllables, do-re-mi-fa-sol-la-ti-do will each be represented by a different bell: C-D-E-F-G-A-B-C. Use colored cue cards corresponding to the colors of the bells with each syllable printed on them to cue each senior performing. Each bell sounds when the group is singing its corresponding syllable in the context of the song. For simplicity, you can use the same bell for both high and low "C." Using the cue cards in this song lays the groundwork for more complicated hand bell patterns, using hand bells to play the melody rather than chordal accompaniments of other songs. For more advanced groups, use the cue cards to lead the melody of the middle verse which goes as follows:

"So do la fa mi do re, so do la ti do re do

When you know the notes to sing,

You can sing most anything!"

Musical Instrument Suggestions

Some instruments can be difficult to identify by ear for those who are not trained musicians. In making my selections for this exercise, I tried to choose instruments that are more easily identifiable by timbre or in relationship to other similar instruments (ex. violin and cello). The following instruments were a good mix for my seniors. I was able to find samples of each instrument soloing on iTunes.

Piano, Acoustic Guitar, Banjo, Flute, Trumpet, Cello, Violin, Drums, Harp, Saxophone

Suggested Musical Genres CD Tracks

(I only use some of these in each group depending on time.)

- "In the Mood" ~ Glenn Miller (Jazz/Big Band)
- "A Night in Tunisha" ~ Dizzy Gillepsie (Jazz/Big Band)
- "I Walk the Line" ~ Johnny Cash (Country-Western)
- "Rock and Roll is Here to Stay" ~ Danny and the Juniors (Rock and Roll)
- "Good Golly Miss Molly" ~ Little Richard (Rock and Roll)
- Beethoven's *Seventh Symphony*, the 3rd Movement (Classical)
- Vivaldi's *Four Seasons*, Largo from "Winter" (Classical)

"In the Mood" is great for use as a movement to music exercise.

"I Walk the Line" or one of the rock and roll songs works well for shaking along with instruments.

Closing Relaxation/Stretching Suggested Movements

Complete each of the following movements several times. Start with some deep breaths. Then stretch arms up towards the ceiling and slowly lower to the sides. Then stretch arms out to the front, then out the sides as if swimming and down. Roll ankles one at a time, flex one foot at a time back towards self and point it to the ground several times. Slowly roll shoulders and end with a few more deep breaths.

OUTLINE: *1950s*

NOTE: *This session contains more than an hour's worth of ideas. Edit it for time accordingly and choose the material that best suits your group's needs, or divide it into two sessions, possibly adding a drum circle to each.*

Opening/Introduce Theme:

Introduce the theme of the 1950s. Pass out a variety of small percussion instruments and have seniors shake along with "**Jamba-laya**," "**Hound Dog**," "*La Bamba*," and "**Rock Around the Clock**."

Movement to Music:

Lead a movement to music exercise with a recording of the song, "**If I Knew You Were Comin' I'd've Baked a Cake**." Give a variety of movement directions throughout the song. See Part Three for ideas.

Group Discussion:

Lead seniors in a discussion about the 1950s. Ask them to share what they remember about the 1950s. Discuss products and inventions, as well as popular culture from the 1950s.

Song Packets and Related Exercises:

Pass out song packets containing lyrics to all of the following songs to each group participant. Sing each song as a group and complete related exercises as indicated. See resources as needed.

- "**The Ballad of Davy Crockett**" (1954)
- "**(How Much is) That Doggie in the Window?**" (1953) – Add cabasas to create the barking sound effects originally featured in the song.
- "**The Tennessee Waltz**" (1950)
- "*Que Sera, Sera*" (1956)
- "**You Belong to Me**" (1952)

- "**That's Amore**" (1953)
- "**Music, Music, Music**" (1950) – Add hand bells and jingle bells and to play on the word "Music."
- "**Hey, Good Lookin'**" (1951)
- "**Walkin' After Midnight**" (1957)

Event Timeline:

Have seniors take turns drawing from an array of cue cards, each with a picture and/or description of an event of the 1950s to share with the group before placing the card in the appropriate place on a 1950s timeline.

Shakeable Instruments:

Pass out two maracas, shakers, or bells to each senior and shake along with two recorded songs.

- "**Rock and Roll Waltz**"– Follow the waltz beat and shake 2x to the right, then 2x to the left, etc.
- "**Mack the Knife**"– Emphasize shaking patterns that use alternating hands.

Boomwhackers:

Introduce the Boomwhackers and play along with two recorded songs, "**The Happy Organ**" and "**Rocking Pneumonia and the Boogie Woogie Flu**." See Part Three for ideas.

Closing:

Lead seniors in a slow movement to music and stretching exercise to a recording of the song, "*Vaya Con Dios*."

ADDITIONAL RESOURCES:

Brief Overview of the 1950s

- After the end of World War II in 1945, the United States experienced an economic boom during the 1950s.
- Television became mainstream and shows such as *I Love Lucy, Leave it to Beaver,* and *The Honeymooners,* were popular.
- The Cold War between the United States and the Soviet Union continued throughout the entire decade.

- Fads of this era included "cramming," attempts to cram as many people as possible into a small space such as a phone booth or Volkswagen.
- Frisbees and Hula Hoops became popular.
- The Civil Rights Movement gained traction.
- Rock and Roll Music emerged and became immensely popular during the second half of the decade.

Famous Products and Inventions of the 1950s

Color Television

First Satellite

Boeing 707 Plane

Power Steering

Laser

JIF Peanut Butter

WD-40

Kentucky Fried Chicken

Pampers Disposable Diapers

Barbie Dolls

Corvettes

Thunderbirds

Play-Doh

Credit Cards

Events of the 1950s

NOTE: *I usually do not do all of these due to time. I pick and choose based on the interests of the group.*

1950 The first "Peanuts" cartoon comic strip appears

1950 Sister Mary Teresa begins her charity work in India and becomes known as Mother Teresa

1951 The TV show, *I Love Lucy*, appears on television

1952 Elizabeth II becomes Queen of the United Kingdom

1952 Car seat belts are introduced

1953 The first Chevy Corvette is built

1953 DNA is discovered

1954 Leonard Bernstein makes his first television appearance

1954 Segregation is ruled illegal in the United States

1955 Disney Land opens in California

1955 Rosa Parks refuses to give up her seat on the bus

1956 Grace Kelly marries Prince Rainier III of Monaco

1956 Elvis Presley first enters the American Music Charts with the song, "Heartbreak Hotel"

1957 The Soviet Satellite, *Sputnik*, launches the Space Age

1958 NASA is founded

1958 Van Cliburn wins the International Tchaikovsky Competition in Moscow

1959 Alaska becomes the 49th U.S. State

1959 Hawaii becomes the 50th U.S. State

OUTLINE: *Thanksgiving*

Opening/Introduce Theme:

Pass out a variety of small percussion instruments and lead seniors in singing and shaking along with a few popular/favorite songs.

Sing **"Shine on, Harvest Moon"** and introduce the theme of "Thanksgiving." Discuss how Thanksgiving marks the end of the harvest season.

Group Discussion:

Discuss Thanksgiving. Ask seniors questions to review the history of the holiday and why we celebrate it. Use more open-ended questions or more leading questions depending on the needs of the group.

Singing/Group Discussion:

Use the group discussion to lead up to the central idea of Thanksgiving being a time to give thanks and "count your blessings." Sing the chorus of the song, **"Count Your Blessings,"** 3x then prompt each senior to share what he or she is thankful for this year. For seniors who say "everything," prompt them to be more specific. For those having difficulty, offer several suggestions for them to choose from such as friends, family, freedom, etc.

Song Packets and Related Exercises:

Pass out song packets containing lyrics to all of the following songs to each group participant. Sing each song as a group and complete related exercises as indicated. See resources as needed.

- **"Over the River and Through the Wood"** – Have seniors share about their family traditions and discuss traditional ways of celebrating Thanksgiving.
- **"Turkey in the Straw"**
- **"Come, Ye Thankful People, Come"**
- **"We Gather Together"**
- **"Yes! We Have No Bananas"** – Sing 2x and collect song packets before starting the songwriting exercise.

Group Songwriting:

After singing the song, **"Yes! We Have No Bananas,"** from the song packets, use that same tune and lead the group in a fill-in-the-blank style songwriting exercise about favorite Thanksgiving foods! Sometimes, I like to do two full verses!

Closing:

Pass out drums and a variety of percussion instruments and lead seniors in a drum circle.

ADDITIONAL RESOURCES:

History of Thanksgiving

Just some key points to keep your discussion on track!

- The Pilgrims left England seeking religious freedom and sailed to America aboard the *Mayflower*.
- They arrived at Plymouth Rock in Massachusetts on December 11, 1620.
- This first winter, between the cold weather and lack of food was devastating.
- The Native Americans helped the Pilgrims in the following spring, teaching them how to effectively grow crops in this new world.
- The harvest of 1621 was a bountiful one. The Pilgrims gathered to give thanks to God and celebrate with a feast. They invited the Native Americans to celebrate with them.
- October, 1777, was the first time all 13 colonies joined together in a Thanksgiving celebration, though it was only a one-time affair.
- Thanksgiving was proclaimed by every United States President after Lincoln, through the date was changed a few times.
- Thanksgiving was sanctioned by Congress in 1941 as a legal, national holiday, annually occurring on the fourth Thursday in November.

"Count Your Blessings" Chorus (from an old hymn by Johnson Oatman, Jr.)

"Count your blessings, name them one by one, Count your blessings, see what God has done! Count your blessings, name them one by one, Count your many blessings, see what God has done!"

Thanksgiving Foods Songwriting

To the tune of "Yes! We Have no Bananas!"

Yes! It's time for Thanksgiving,

It's time for Thanksgiving today!

We'll eat_____and_____

_____and_____and_____

And all sorts of fruit and say-

We'll eat_____and_____and_____

_____and_____and_____

And Yes! It's time for Thanksgiving,

It's time for Thanksgiving today!

OUTLINE: *Holidays*

NOTE: *I usually do all Christmas music throughout the month of December, but like to use this session for the groups I have between Thanksgiving and December 1st. I feel it is too early to really start celebrating the Christmas holidays, but Thanksgiving is already over so this session helps to bridge that gap while still maintaining the holiday spirit. This session repeats some ideas from the "Thanksgiving" session plan, so I only do it with groups with which I DID NOT already do the Thanksgiving session plan.*

Opening:

Pass out drums and a variety of percussion instruments and lead seniors in a drum circle.

Group Discussion:

Discuss Thanksgiving briefly, reviewing the history of Thanksgiving and why we celebrate it. Discuss Thanksgiving as the start of the holiday season, a general time of thankfulness. Use the discussion to lead into the next song.

Singing/Group Discussion:

Use the group discussion to lead up to the central idea of the holidays being a joyful time of celebrating the good things in your life and for experiencing gratitude. Sing the chorus of the song, **"Count Your Blessings,"** 3x, then prompt each senior to share what they are thankful for this year. For seniors who say "everything" prompt them to be more specific. For those having difficulty offer several suggestions such as friends, family, freedom, etc.

Song Packets and Related Exercises:

Pass out song packets containing lyrics to all of the following songs to each group participant. Sing each song as a group and complete related exercises as indicated. See resources as needed.

- **"Over the River and Through the Wood"**– Have seniors share about their family holiday traditions and discuss traditional ways of celebrating the holidays.

- **"My Favorite Things"**– Have each senior name a favorite thing about the holiday season.
- **"What a Wonderful World"**
- **"Yes! We Have No Bananas"**– Sing 2x and collect song packets before starting the songwriting exercise.

Group Songwriting:

After singing the song, **"Yes! We Have No Bananas,"** from the song packets, use that same tune and lead the group in a fill-in-the-blank style songwriting exercise about favorite holiday foods! Sometimes, I like to do two full verses!

Closing:

Lead seniors in singing along with two popular Christmas songs, **"Jingle Bells"** and **"Deck the Halls."**

- **"Jingle Bells"**– Pass out bells to one side of the group and maracas to the other. Prompt seniors with the maracas to only play along during the verses. Prompt seniors with the bells to only play during the chorus. Briefly review when each section starts and stops playing. Then sing the song as a group 1-2x with the instruments adding to the accompaniment.
- **"Deck the Halls"**– Sing the song as a group and have seniors shake along with instruments.

ADDITIONAL RESOURCES:

History of Thanksgiving/Start of the Holiday Season Discussion Points

Just some key points to keep your discussion on track!

- The Pilgrims left England seeking religious freedom and sailed to America aboard the *Mayflower*.
- They arrived at Plymouth Rock in Massachusetts on December 11, 1620.
- This first winter, between the cold weather and lack of food was devastating.
- The Native Americans helped the Pilgrims in the following spring, teaching them how to effectively grow crops in this new world.
- The harvest of 1621 was a bountiful one. The Pilgrims gathered to give thanks to God and celebrate with a feast. They invited the Native Americans to celebrate with them.
- The holiday season is generally seen as starting with Thanksgiving and upcoming holidays include Christmas, Hanukkah, New Year's, etc.
- The holiday season is often viewed as a time for gratitude, peace, joy, and love.
- Holiday traditions and ways to celebrate may include: seeing friends and family; gathering for a feast; baking Christmas cookies; decorating a Christmas tree; hanging lights outside the house; singing Christmas carols; eating special foods; exchanging gifts; going to parties, etc.

"Count Your Blessings" Chorus (from an old hymn by Johnson Oatman, Jr.)

"Count your blessings, name them one by one, Count your blessings, see what God has done!
Count your blessings, name them one by one, Count your many blessings, see what God has done!"

Holiday Foods Songwriting

To the tune of "Yes! We Have No Bananas!"

Yes! Let's Celebrate the Season,

The Holiday Season is here!

We'll eat_____and_____

_____and_____and_____

And all sorts of sweets and say-

We'll eat_____and_____and_____

_____and_____and_____

And Yes! Let's Celebrate the Season,

The Holiday Season is here!

OUTLINE: *Christmas* I

Opening:

Lead seniors in singing along with two popular Christmas songs, **"Jingle Bells"** and *"Feliz Navidad."*

- **"Jingle Bells"**– Pass out bells to one side of the group and maracas to the other. Prompt seniors with the maracas to only play along during the verses. Prompt seniors with the bells to only play during the chorus. Briefly review when each section starts and stops playing. Then sing the song as a group 1x or 2x with the instruments adding to the accompaniment.
- *"Feliz Navidad"*– Sing the song as a group and have seniors shake along with instruments.

Instrumental Performance:

Introduce the song, **"The Twelve Days of Christmas."** I usually sing just the first verse to jog everyone's memory before saying that today the group is going to use instruments to create their own special version of the song. Ask for volunteers (or prompt individuals, some folks need extra encouragement!) to musically represent each of the 12 days/12 gifts indicated in the song. Depending on the group dynamics/abilities, either assign instruments or give each volunteer a choice of instruments to play during their line. With larger groups, have more than one senior play each part so everyone who wants to have a part can have one. I have a cue card for each verse to help everyone remember on which line they play. Start with just the first verse and have the first volunteer practice playing on cue, to help the group understand the idea. Then pass out three or four more instrumental parts, then stop and practice just that much, before adding three or four more instrumental parts and stopping to practice. After all 12 parts have been assigned, practice as a group just the last verse (starting with "Twelve drummers drumming") until everyone is comfortable with their part and playing on cue fairly consistently. Then sing the entire song together as a group with each instrument playing at the appropriate time. Sometimes after finishing the song, the group may enjoy trying just the last verse again going faster and faster, or with more advanced groups take away each person's cue card and use this as a memory exercise to see if the group can remember the order of verses and when to play.

Song Packets and Related Exercises:

Pass out song packets (or use Christmas Songbooks) containing lyrics to all of the following songs to each group participant. Sing each song as a group.

- **"Deck the Halls"**
- **"Jolly Old Saint Nicholas"**
- **"Rudolph, The Red-Nosed Reindeer"**
- **"Silent Night"**
- **"We Wish You A Merry Christmas"**

Closing:

Lead a movement to music exercise with a recording of the song, **"The Merry Christmas Polka."** Give a variety of movement directions throughout the song. See Part Three for ideas.

ADDITIONAL RESOURCES:

"The Twelve Days of Christmas"

Instrument Suggestions

A Partridge in a Pear Tree ~ Wooden Monk Bell or Tambourine

2 Turtle Doves ~ Seed Shakers or Shekere

3 French Hens ~ Cabasa

4 Calling Birds ~ Castanets/Wooden Clapper

5 Golden Rings ~ Hand Bell

6 Geese-a-Laying ~ Maracas or Shakers

7 Swans-a-Swimming ~ Clatterpillar

8 Maids-a-Milking ~ Triangle

9 Ladies Dancing ~ Jingle Bells

10 Lords -a- Leaping ~ Cymbals

11 Pipers Piping ~ Slide Whistles

12 Drummers Drumming ~ Paddle Drum/Hand Drum

Christmas Song Packets/Songbooks

I made my own Christmas Songbooks that contain about 50 Christmas songs and a table of contents. My copy has chords, while those for the seniors have lyrics only. For some groups I use these books and take requests. For others I use the song packets containing the songs listed, which I have found to be generally well-known and loved. Suggested Christmas Songbook contents can be found in Part Three. Please note that song lyrics are protected under copyright law and use careful consideration when using printed versions of lyrics. Many of the songs suggested for the Christmas song-books are not considered in the public domain so please be sure your use of all copyrighted materials falls under the guide-lines of fair use.

OUTLINE: *Christmas* II

Opening:

Pass out Christmas songbooks and take requests of favorite Christmas songs and sing them together as a group.

Name That Tune:

Play a recording of instrumental versions of some popular Christmas songs and see if seniors can identify the song, before singing it together as a group. I use my Christmas Songbooks for this, though song packets containing all of the lyrics would work as well. iTunes is a great resource for finding instrumental versions to use with this exercise.

Drumming and Group Discussion:

Sing the song, "**Little Drummer Boy**," adding a group accompaniment pattern on the drums. Use just a steady beat for seniors who are lower functioning and a long-short-long-short (think dotted quarter note, eighth note, dotted quarter note, eighth note) for seniors who are higher functioning. Then lead a group discussion about gifts. Ask seniors to share about a favorite or most memorable gift they have received. Then discuss how the drummer boy in the song did not have money for a gift, but was able to give the gift of music. Ask seniors about gifts they can share or give to others that do not cost much money (i.e. homemade cookies, handmade Christmas cards, sewing/knitting something, etc.)

Group Songwriting:

Sing the song, "**We Wish You a Merry Christmas**," then use the tune for a group songwriting exercise, singing about favorite Christmas foods and Christmas traditions. Sing several verses, each including a different holiday tradition and different favorite holiday food.

Closing:

Pass out a variety of instruments and have seniors shake along with a recording of the song, "**Rockin' Around the Christmas Tree**" and/or "**Jingle Bell Rock**."

ADDITIONAL RESOURCES:

"We Wish You a Merry Christmas" Songwriting

We wish you a Merry Christmas

We wish you a Merry Christmas

We wish you a Merry Christmas and a Happy New Year!

Oh bring us some ___(insert holiday food)___ (3x)

And a cup of good cheer!

We won't go until ___(insert tradition or way to celebrate)___ (3x)

And celebrate today!

We wish you a Merry Christmas

We wish you a Merry Christmas

We wish you a Merry Christmas and a Happy New Year!

Holiday Foods Examples

Hot Chocolate

Christmas Cookies

Turkey and Dressing

Ham and Potatoes

Pie and Ice Cream

Etc.

Holiday Traditions Examples

Decorate the Tree

Open Presents

Sing Christmas Carols

See the (Christmas) Lights

Hang up Stockings

Etc.

Christmas Songbooks

I created my own Christmas Songbooks for use throughout the month of December. The table of contents with suggested songs is included in Part Three. Please note that song lyrics are protected under copyright law and use careful consideration when using printed versions of lyrics. Many of the songs suggested are not considered in the public domain so please be sure your use of all copyrighted materials falls under the guidelines of fair use.

Christmas ADDITIONAL IDEAS

NOTE: *I have yet to work in a community or day program where any of the seniors celebrate Kwanza, Hanukkah, or a December holiday other than Christmas. Christmas music remains immensely popular with all of my groups and I make a habit of doing Christmas music exclusively throughout the entire month of December. However, I do check with each community ahead of time to be sure Christmas music will be appropriate.*

Singing-Unusual Christmas Songs:

Teach seniors a new or unusual Christmas song and sing it together. Seniors tend to get a kick out of such songs as **"Dominick the Donkey," "I Want A Hippopotamus for Christmas,"** or **"I'm Getting Nuttin' for Christmas."**

- **"Dominick the Donkey"** – Practice vocally emphasizing the "hee haw" part or add instruments and play call and response style on the "clippity clop hee haw hee haw" part. For example, have seniors play the drums on "clippity clop" and play the slide whistles on "hee haw."
- **"I'm Getting Nuttin' For Christmas"** – Have seniors discuss some of the pranks or mischief they pulled when they were young.
- **"I Want A Hippopotamus for Christmas"** – Have seniors discuss if they ever requested or received an unusual or outrageous gift for Christmas.

Hand Bells:

Have seniors play the accompaniment for the song, **"Silver Bells,"** using the hand bells to form chords.

Movement to Music Using Scarves:

Pass out scarves for seniors to move and wave along with a song such as **"Blue Christmas,"** or a selection from the *Nutcracker* ballet.

Group Discussion:

Discuss some of the stories behind famous Christmas songs and then sing those songs together.

The book, *Stories Behind the Best-Loved Songs of Christmas*, by Ace Collins may be a good resource.

Group Discussion:

Sing the song, **"I'll Be Home for Christmas,"** and discuss the difficulty of being away from home during the holiday season. Have seniors share favorite traditions and memories of their family Christmas celebrations and then discuss things they enjoy about celebrating the season in their current community with their friends.

Additional Resources

PART THREE

INSTRUMENT EXTRAVAGANZA

In addition to doing theme-based sessions with my seniors, I love to mix it up and do some sessions that focus exclusively on drumming, playing a variety of instruments, and movement. These sessions are affectionately known as "instrument extravaganzas!" Below are simple suggestions and some ideas of songs to use when seeking to incorporate a variety of instruments.

Ocean Drum:

Demonstrate several ways to play the ocean drum and give seniors a chance to experiment and see what sort of different sounds each group member can create.

Have seniors take turns providing an accompaniment on the ocean drum as the groups sings one or more songs. I usually ask for a different volunteer to drum along with each verse. Below are some of my favorite "water-themed" songs to use with the ocean drum.

- "On Moonlight Bay"
- "My Bonnie Lies Over the Ocean"
- "Michael, Row the Boat Ashore"
- "Singin' in the Rain"
- "Beyond the Reef"
- "On the Good Ship Lollipop"

Egg Shakers/Conga Shakers:

Add a rhythmic shaking pattern to accompany a song. Demonstrate and practice the wrist movements (twist the wrist like opening a doorknob) necessary to create a strong-weak (or strong-weak-weak, depending on the rhythm of the song) beat pattern using conga shakers or egg shakers. Practice keeping the beat as a group. Follow the rhythm and shake along while singing. It can be fun to do it one time for practice and then try to go faster and faster! Though the list of suggestions is endless, below are some song suggestions that are generally well-known and a lot of fun with an added rhythmic accompaniment.

- "Yes Sir, That's My Baby"
- "I've Been Working on the Railroad"/"The Eyes of Texas"
- "Don't Sit Under the Apple Tree"
- "Won't You Come Home, Bill Bailey"
- "There's A Tavern in the Town"

Maracas and Bells:

Divide the group into two sections—one playing the maracas and one playing the bells. Instruct one section to play during the verse and the other during the chorus of a well-known or favorite song. Sing the song call and response style, allowing the instruments to accentuate the lyrics of the song.

For example, in the song, "Jingle Bells," have the maracas play during the verses ("Dashing through the snow...") and the bells during the chorus ("Jingle bells, jingle bells..."). "Jingle Jangle Jingle" is another good example for using bells during the chorus ("I've got spurs that jingle jangle jingle...") and the maracas during the verses, but really the possibilities are endless.

All Things Shakeable: (Maracas, Bells, Tambourines, Shakers, etc.)

Sing a popular song and then add movement/ shaking directions, using a song such as "Rock Around the Clock," as explained in the Introductory Session outline. Other songs could be used for this sort of activity as well.

Sing a song adding in starts and stops and dramatic pauses. Instruct seniors to play while you play and sing, and to stop when you stop. After a few verses when everyone is comfortable, start changing where the stops and starts occur in the song, change the lengths of the stops, or maybe gesture as if you are going to start playing again (but don't) to "catch" who is paying attention. My seniors really love doing this and one of my favorite songs for this activity is "Jailhouse Rock."

Sing a song and instruct seniors to shake fast when you play fast, slow when you play slow, and loud and soft when you play loud and soft. This has been another big hit with several of my groups and one of my favorite songs for this activity is "Hound Dog."

Boomwhackers:

I'll admit I was completely nervous about trying to integrate this rather funky instrument into sessions with my seniors. But my seniors universally LOVE them! They are incorporated in a few of the themed sessions as well. Some basic activities may include playing them on the beat of an upbeat, recorded (so you can model) song such as "See you Later, Alligator." I like to then add directions to play up high, down on the floor, on a wheelchair or chair or table, play with a neighbor, play by yourself, etc. throughout the song. Another favorite, is playing along with the *Addam's Family* theme song, following the rhythmic pattern, see the Halloween Session outline.

Boomwhackers are also great for promoting exercise. Have seniors play with a partner for some range of motion work. One senior moves his/her boomwhackers as a sort of moving target for his/her partner to hit. After awhile, have seniors switch roles.

Play along with a song and have seniors play on the floor on each side of their chairs, on the floor in front of their chairs, and then up high for some great for range of motion work as well.

I also like to do some songs with volume variations, instructing seniors to hit the boomwhackers hard to play loudly, then lightly to play softly. We also sometimes do tempo variations and demonstrate the tempo changes by varying our movements (think Eurythmics). At a slower tempo, we make big and wide movements between each hit and at a faster tempo we make short, small movements between each hit.

"Duke of Earl" is another boomwhacker favorite with my seniors. We divide the group into two sections. One section uses the Boomwhackers to keep the beat during the verses and the second section uses the cabasas to add some rhythmic pizzazz during the chorus, while playing along with a recording of the song.

Cabasas:

We occasionally use the cabasas to add a rhythmic accompaniment to a recorded or live-performed song. Some great songs for cabasas include: "Under the Boardwalk," "Stand By Me," and "Fever."

Hand Bells:

Many of the themed sessions contain interventions using hand bell chords to create an accompaniment for a song. With some of my more advanced groups, I like to work on using the hand bells to perform the melodies of popular songs. To introduce this concept, I used color-coded cards, which coordinate with the color of each bell, to lay out the notes of the melody on a large chart. I point to each card when it is time for that bell to play. With advanced groups that have mastered playing melodies in this way, teaching basic rhythmic notation (quarter, half notes, etc.) is a great possibility, while still color-coding the notes to indicate pitch.

Movement to Music:

Adding one or two movement to music exercises can round out a session devoted to instruments and drumming. I usually like to end this sort of session with a stretching/relaxation exercise and some deep breathing. Depending on the group, adding an upbeat movement to music exercise at the start of the session can serve as a nice warm-up as well.

DRUMMING IDEAS

There are many great resources available that are specifically devoted to drumming and how to successfully incorporate drumming into music therapy sessions, so this section will serve as a very brief introduction and offer just a few suggestions. While many of my seniors would have a tough time drumming for the entirety of a session, all of them LOVE the drums. We frequently drum as a part of our themed sessions. We also do sessions with a lot of drumming, but with movement activities, instrument playing, and a few songs mixed in as well. Below are a few ideas for leading a drum circle and/or incorporating drumming into music therapy sessions with your seniors.

Body Percussion:

Body percussion can be a fun, rhythmic warm-up to drumming. Create a rhythmic pattern that is performed on and with the body using the following four actions: stomp feet, pat knees (seniors are seated so this will be your lap) clap hands, snap fingers above the head. Since each action is also organized vertically, it will add an additional layer of cuing. Create rhythms from these four basic motions and have seniors see if they can repeat them back. This is excellent not just for rhythmic work, but also as a cognitive exercise. Some seniors may have trouble snapping and

that motion can be modified to a finger clap/soft clap for them. Also give seniors a chance to lead, demonstrating rhythms for the group to repeat using this method as well.

Rhythm Practice:

Using drums (and other rhythmic percussion instruments as desired) practice replicating rhythms. Play a rhythm on the drum and have seniors play it back. Progress from short, simple rhythmic patterns to longer and more challenging patterns depending on the abilities of the group. Also have seniors take turns leading and creating patterns for the group to replicate as well.

Drums and Songs:

Have seniors drum along with a song. This can be as simple as keeping a steady beat while singing a song such as, "I've Been Working on the Railroad," or following the more complex rhythm of a piece of classical music such as a selection from *Peer Gynt* by Grieg or *Carmen* by Bizet. One of Sousa's marches, or a jazzy selection from the 1930s are other possibilities.

Isolate different instruments in the form of a song. I like to do, "Hail, Hail, the Gang's All Here," as a greeting song, but change it to, "Hail Hail we've got (*maracas, or drums, or bells, or whatever*) and have everyone with that type of instrument play when we sing about it.

Add drum rolls to a song. I love using the song, "Farewell Ladies, Farewell Gentlemen," as a closing song while the group gives a drum roll each time we sing, "roll along."

Drum Circle:

For drum circles with my seniors, I use drums (hand and paddle) in addition to a variety of other small percussion instruments. Especially when drumming is less familiar to a group, I lead on a paddle drum and establish a strong rhythmic basis, moving my arms up higher to indicate it is time to play louder and moving my arms lower to indicate playing softer. As a group, we'll do a variety of crescendos and decrescendos, sudden louds and sudden softs, etc. Once the group is comfortable with drumming in general and this basic format, we'll add some of the following variations.

* Ask for volunteers (or prompt someone) to take a turn leading the group. Many of my seniors have been hesitant at first, but with a little encouragement and reassurance, end up doing an amazing job and having a lot of fun!

* Split the group into two sections. Whichever group is facing the therapist plays, while the section to the therapist's back listens. Switch back and forth between which section is playing, sometimes giving each section a longer chance to drum and sometimes switching between the two groups very rapidly. It's fun to hear the two groups answering back and forth with the drums. This is also a great way for seniors to get to hear what their friends are doing and then provide encouragement and feedback to one another.

* Stop the group ensemble while gesturing to one senior to keep playing before bringing the group back in to give each senior a chance to do a solo.

* Isolate different instruments (i.e. drums, bells, maracas, boomwhackers) to give each instrument section a solo. Depending on the strengths and needs of a group, possibly use cue cards or seat seniors by instrument type (rather than having all the instruments interspersed throughout the group) to make it easier.

* Do a "rhythm machine" with smaller groups. Start with only one person playing and add in players one at a time until the entire group is playing together. Then have one person at a time stop playing until the entire group is silent. This can be a fun way to layer sounds and rhythms.

* Have seniors swap instruments at different stopping points to encourage them to try as many different instruments as possible and to encourage interaction with their fellow group members.

MOVEMENT IDEAS

 For Movement to Music Exercises

All movements can be completed while seated.

Lower Extremities:

- Tap Toes
- Tap Toes Side to Side (twisting at the ankle, move toes together to the right and to the left)
- Tap Heels
- Tap Heels Side to Side (twisting from the toes, move heels together to the right and to the left)
- Alternate between Tapping Toes and Heels (both toes and heels landing at the same time)
- Alternate between Tapping Toes and Heels (one foot's toes and one foot's heel landing at the same time)
- Extend Leg Forward and Tap Toe (alternate between each leg)
- Extend Leg Forward and Tap Heel (alternate between each leg)
- Kicks (alternate between each leg)
- Turn Toes Out and In
- Turn Heels Out and In
- Alternate Between a Toe Tap and a Kick
- Move one foot out to the side and then back in towards the center (alternate between the feet)
- Move one foot forward and then back in towards the center (alternate between the feet)
- March in Place

For Movement to Music Exercises (continued)

All movements can be completed while seated.

Upper Body:
- Sway Side to Side
- Shake Shoulders
- Raise and Lower Shoulders Together
- Raise and Lower Alternating Shoulders
- While shaking shoulders lean forwards slowly, then straighten back up
- Clap Hands
- Pat Knees
- Alternate between Clapping Hands and Patting Knees
- Move Elbows Out and In
- Roll Arms
- Swing Arms (forwards and backwards)
- Swing Arms (side to side)
- Alternate between Patting Knees and Tapping Shoulders
- Pat Knees and Tap Alternating Shoulders Crossing Midline (one hand at a time)
- Pat Knees and Tap Alternating Shoulders Crossing Midline (both hands at the same time)
- Wave Hands/Jazz Hands

For Shakeable Instrument Exercises

All movements can be completed while seated.

- Shake up high and down low towards the floor
- Shake forward and back (arms stretched out in front and back close to the body)
- Shake side to side as if doing the twist
- Shake with both arms to one side, then both arms to the other side like hula dancing
- Shake while moving arms around in a big circle
- Shake with one hand high and one hand low and keep alternating hands
- Shake with one hand forward and one hand back towards the body and keep alternating hands
- Shake with both arms out to the sides, then bring arms in towards the middle
- Have seniors demonstrate a shaking pattern for the group to imitate
- Shake as fast as possible, like a "rumble"

POPULAR/FAVORITE SONGS FOR SENIORS

The following songs have proven to be generally well-known by many/most seniors in my groups (without the aid of songbooks) and are my go-to songs for opening a group, getting everyone warmed up and engaged, etc. Of course there are many other popular songs your seniors may know by heart as well. This list is here to provide a starting point.

"Alexander's Ragtime Band"
"America the Beautiful"
"Bicycle Built for Two"
"By the Light of the Silvery Moon"
"Deep in the Heart of Texas"
"Don't Sit Under the Apple Tree"
"Eyes of Texas, The"
"Five Foot Two, Eyes of Blue"
"God Bless America"
"Hail, Hail the Gang's All Here"
"He's Got the Whole World in His Hands"
"Hey, Good Lookin'"
"Home on the Range"
"Hound Dog"
"(How Much is) That Doggie in the Window"
"I Could Have Danced All Night"
"I've Been Working on the Railroad"
"Jambalaya"
"Jingle Jangle Jingle"
"La Bamba"
"Let Me Call You Sweetheart"
"Music, Music, Music" ("Put Another Nickel In")
"My Blue Heaven"

"My Bonnie Lies Over the Ocean"
"Oh! Susanna"
"Oh, What a Beautiful Morning"
"Old Time Religion"
"On Moonlight Bay"
"Que Sera, Sera"
"She'll Be Coming 'Round the Mountain"
"Shine On, Harvest Moon"
"Side By Side"
"Take Me Home, Country Roads"
"Take Me Out to the Ballgame"
"Tennessee Waltz, The"
"There's A Tavern in the Town"
"This Land is Your Land"
"This Little Light of Mine"
"When the Saints Go Marching In"
"Won't You Come Home, Bill Bailey"
"Yankee Doodle"
"Yellow Rose of Texas, The"
"Yes Sir, That's My Baby"
"You Are My Sunshine"
"You're a Grand Old Flag"
"Zip-A Dee-Doo-Dah"

CHRISTMAS SONGBOOK

Suggested Contents

*Most Popular/Most Easily Recognized Songs are in **bold***

"Angels We Have Heard on High"
"Auld Lang Syne"
"Away in a Manger"
"Blue Christmas"
"Christmas in Killarney"
"Coventry Carol"
"Deck the Halls"
"Dominick the Donkey"
"Do You Hear What I Hear? "
"Feliz Navidad"
"First Noel, The"
"Friendly Beasts, The"
"Frosty the Snowman"
"God Rest Ye Merry Gentlemen"
"Good Christian Men, Rejoice"
"Good King Wenceslas"
"Go, Tell it on the Mountain"
"Hark! The Herald Angels Sing"
"Have Yourself a Merry Little Christmas"
"Here Comes Santa Claus"
"Here We Come A-wassailing"
"Holly and the Ivy, The"
"I'm Getting Nuttin' for Christmas"
"I Saw Three Ships"
"It Came Upon A Midnight Clear"

"I Want a Hippopotamus for Christmas"
"Jingle Bells"
"Jingle Bell Rock"
"Jolly Old Saint Nicholas"
"Joy to the World"
"Let It Snow, Let It Snow, Let It Snow"
"Little Drummer Boy"
"Lo, How a Rose E'er Blooming"
"O Christmas Tree"
"O Come, All Ye Faithful"
"O Come, O Come, Emmanuel"
"O Holy Night"
"O Little Town of Bethlehem"
"Pretty Paper"
"Rockin' Around the Christmas Tree"
"Rudolph, The Red-Nosed Reindeer"
"Santa Claus is Coming to Town"
"Silent Night"
"Silver Bells"
"Twelve Days of Christmas, The"
"Up on the Housetop"
"We Three Kings of Orient Are"
"We Wish You a Merry Christmas"
"What Child is This?"
"White Christmas"

FAVORITE PLAYLISTS/CDS

iTunes and other such programs have made creating custom mix-CDs or playlists for your senior groups unbelievably easy. I actually prefer creating my own mixes over buying CDs as it allows me to hand select the numbers that I think will be most popular with my seniors and work the best for a variety of interventions. Here are some of my favorite go-to CDs/playlists.

1920s Disk A

1) "Swanee" ~ Al Jolson 1920

2) "Charleston" ~ Paul Whiteman 1925

3) "Pinetop's Boogie Woogie" ~ Pinetop Smith 1928

4) "I Want to be Loved by You" ~ Helen Kane 1928

5) "Sweet Georgia Brown" ~ Ben Bernie 1926

6) "Muskrat Ramble" ~ Louis Armstrong 1926

7) "Ain't Misbehavin'" ~ Fats Waller 1929

8) "My Blue Heaven" ~ Gene Austin 1927

9) "Baby Face" ~ Jan Garber and His Orchestra 1926

10) "Carolina in the Morning" ~ Al Jolson 1923

11) "West End Blues" ~ Louis Armstrong 1928

12) "In the Jailhouse Now" ~ Jimmie Rodgers 1928

13) "Nobody Knows You When You're Down and Out" ~ Bessie Smith 1923

14) "Tiptoe Through the Tulips" ~ Nick Lucas 1929

15) "April Showers" ~ Al Jolson 1921

16) "Heebie Jeebies" ~ Louis Armstrong 1926

17) "It Had to Be You" ~ Isham Jones and Gus Kahn 1924

18) "Toot, Toot, Tootsie! Goodbye" ~ Al Jolson 1922

1920s Disk B

1) "King Porter Stomp" ~ Jelly Roll Morton 1923 (later made famous by Benny Goodman)

2) "When the Red, Red Robin Comes Bob, Bob Bobbin' Along" ~ Al Jolson 1926

3) "Black and Tan Fantasy" ~ Duke Ellington 1929

4) "T'ain't Nobody's Business If I Do" ~ Bessie Smith 1922 (I prefer the version by Dinah Washington)

5) "Someone to Watch Over Me" ~ Gertrude Lawrence 1926 (I prefer the version by Ella Fitzgerald)

6) "My Man" ~ Fanny Brice 1922

7) "See See Rider Blues" ~ Ma Rainey 1924

8) "In a Mist" ~ Bix Beiderbecke 1927

9) "California, Here I Come" ~ Al Jolson 1921

10) "Let's Do It (Let's Fall in Love) " ~ Dorsey Brothers & Their Orchestra 1928

11) "Keep on the Sunny Side" ~ The Carter Family 1928

12) *Rhapsody in Blue* (original version) ~ George Gershwin 1924

1930s Disk A

1) "In the Mood" ~ Glenn Miller 1939

2) "Sing, Sing, Sing" ~ Benny Goodman 1937

3) "Minnie the Moocher" ~ Cab Calloway 1931

4) "Moonlight Serenade" ~ Glenn Miller 1939

5) "Inka Dinka Doo" ~ Jimmy Durante 1934

6) "Mood Indigo" ~ Duke Ellington 1930

7) "Cheek to Cheek" ~ Fred Astaire 1935

8) "Heartaches" ~ Ted Weems 1933

9) "Begin the Beguine" ~ Artie Shaw 1935 (1938)

10) "Beer Barrel Polka" ~ Will Glahe 1939

11) "If I Didn't Care" ~ The Ink Spots 1939

12) "The Object of My Affection" ~ The Boswell Sisters 1935

13) "Goody Goody" ~ Benny Goodman 1936

14) "Back in the Saddle Again" ~ Gene Autry 1939

15) "One O'Clock Jump" ~ Count Basie 1937

16) "Wabash Cannonball" ~ Roy Acuff 1936

17) "Stompin' at the Savoy" ~ Benny Goodman 1934

18) "Tea for Two" ~ Art Tatum (1925 original) 1939

19) *Bei Mir Bistu Schien* ~ Benny Goodman 1932

1930s Disk B

1) "It Don't Mean a Thing if it Ain't Got that Swing" ~ Duke Ellington 1931
2) "Boogie Woogie" ~ Tommy Dorsey Orchestra 1938
3) "The Flat Foot Floogee" ~ The Mills Brothers 1938
4) "The Peanut Vendor" ~ Sam Browne 1937
5) "Moonglow" ~ Benny Goodman 1933/1934
6) "Thanks for the Memory" ~ Bob Hope 1938
7) "Tiger Rag" ~ The Mills Brothers 1931
8) "It's a Sin to Tell a Lie" ~ Fats Waller 1936
9) "Pennies From Heaven" ~ Bing Crosby 1936
10) "I'm In the Mood For Love" ~ Louis Armstrong 1935
11) "Strange Fruit" ~ Billie Holiday 1939
12) "You Must Have Been a Beautiful Baby" ~ Bing Crosby 1938
13) "I'm Getting Sentimental Over You" ~ Tommy Dorsey 1932
14) "Smoke Gets In Your Eyes" ~ Paul Whiteman 1933
15) "Body and Soul" ~ Coleman Hawkins 1939
16) "Lullaby of Broadway" ~ The Dorsey Brothers 1935/1936

Dance Songs

1) "Shout" ~ The Isley Brothers
2) "The Twist" ~ Chubby Checker
3) "Shake, Rattle and Roll" ~ Bill Haley and His Comets
4) "Twist and Shout" ~ The Isley Brothers
5) "Y.M.C.A." ~ The Village People
6) "Celebration" ~ Kool and the Gang
7) "Electric Boogie (Slide)" ~ Marcia Griffiths
8) "Stayin' Alive" ~ The Bee Gees
9) "Cotton-Eyed Joe" ~ The Moody Brothers
10) "The Chicken Dance" ~ Various Artists
11) "Let's Face the Music and Dance" ~ Frank Sinatra
12) "New York, New York" ~ Frank Sinatra

1940s

1) "Take the "A" Train" ~ Duke Ellington 1941
2) "A String of Pearls" ~ Glenn Miller 1941
3) "Chattanooga Choo-Choo" ~ Glenn Miller 1941
4) "Old Devil Moon" ~ Ella Logan & Donald Richards 1947 (I prefer the version by Frank Sinatra)
5) "Swinging On A Star" ~ Bing Crosby 1944
6) "Boogie Woogie Bugle Boy" ~ The Andrews Sisters 1941
7) "Stormy Weather" ~ Lena Horne 1943
8) "Paper Doll" ~ The Mills Brothers 1943
9) "A Night In Tunisia" ~ Dizzy Gillespie 1942
10) "We Three (My Echo, My Shadow, and Me)" ~ The Ink Spots 1940
11) "Rum and Coca-Cola" ~ The Andrews Sisters 1945
12) "Peg O My Heart" ~ Buddy Clark 1947
13) "Nature Boy" ~ Nat "King" Cole 1948
15) "Some Enchanted Evening" ~ Perry Como (preferred version) 1949
16) "You Always Hurt the One You Love" ~ The Mills Brothers 1944
17) "I've Got a Gal In Kalamazoo" ~ Glenn Miller Orchestra 1942
18) "Riders in the Sky" ~ Vaughn Monroe 1949
19) "Pistol Packin' Mama" ~ The Andrews Sisters 1943
20) "Smoke! Smoke! Smoke (That Cigarette)" ~ Tex Williams 1947
21) "Praise the Lord and Pass the Ammunition" ~ The Merry Macs 1942
22) *Der Fuehrer's* Face" ~ Spike Jones 1943

Doo-Wop Hits

1) "In the Still of the Night" ~ The Five Satins
2) "Sixteen Candles" ~ The Crests
3) "You Belong to Me" ~ The Duprees
4) "Little Darlin'" ~ The Diamonds
5) "At the Hop" ~ Danny & the Juniors
6) "Book of Love" ~ The Monotones
7) "Why Do Fools Fall in Love" ~ Franki Lymon & The Teenagers
8) "Rama Lama Ding Dong" ~ The Edsels
9) "The Lion Sleeps Tonight" ~ The Tokens
10) "Duke of Earl" ~ Gene Chandler

1950s Disk A

1) "The Ballad of Davy Crockett" ~ The Wellingtons 1954

2) "Sixteen Tons" ~ Tennessee Ernie Ford 1955

3) "If I Knew You Were Comin' I'd've Baked a Cake" ~ Eileen Barton 1950

4) "(How Much is) That Doggie in the Window" ~ Patti Page 1953

5) "Hoop-Dee-Doo" ~ Perry Como 1950

6) "Rags to Riches" ~ Tony Bennett 1953

7) "Mack the Knife" ~ Bobby Darin (1928 original) 1959

8) "This Ole House" ~ Rosemary Clooney 1954

9) "The Happy Organ" ~ Dave "Baby" Cotez 1959

10) *La Bamba* ~ Ritchie Valens 1958

11) "Tequila" ~ The Champs 1958

12) "I Walk the Line" ~ Johnny Cash 1956

13) "Folsom Prison Blues" ~ Johnny Cash 1955

14) "The Fat Man" ~ Fats Domino 1950 (recorded 1949, released 1950)

15) "(Let Me Be Your)" Teddy Bear ~ Elvis Presley 1957

16) "Heartbreak Hotel" ~ Elvis Presley 1956

17) "Lawdy Miss Clawdy" ~ Lloyd Price 1952

18) "Long Tall Sally" ~ Little Richard 1956

19) "Love Potion No. 9" ~ The Clovers 1959

20) "Money (That's What I Want)" ~ Barrett Strong 1959

21) "Money Honey" ~ The Drifters 1953

22) "Mr. Sandman" ~ The Chordettes 1954

23) "Rocking Pneumonia and the Boogie Woogie Flu" ~ Huey "Piano" Smith & the Clowns 1957

24) "Sh-Boom" ~ The Chords 1954

25) "Speedoo" ~ The Cadillacs 1955

26) "Maybellene" ~ Chuck Berry 1955

27) "Wake Up Little Susie" ~ The Everly Brothers 1957

28) "Roll Over Beethoven" ~ Chuck Berry 1956

29) "Shake, Rattle and Roll" ~ Bill Haley and His Comets 1954

Three Rock Legends

1) "Oh Boy!" ~ Buddy Holly

2) "Come On, Let's Go" ~ Ritchie Valens

3) "White Lightening" ~ Big Bopper

4) "Crazy Blues" ~ Big Bopper

5) "Peggy Sue" ~ Buddy Holly

6) "Paddiwack Song" ~ Ritchie Valens

7) "That'll Be the Day" ~ Buddy Holly

8) "Chantilly Lace" ~ Big Bopper

9) "Oh Donna" ~ Ritchie Valens

1950s Disk B

1) "Auf Wiederseh'n, Sweetheart" ~ Vera Lynn 1952

2) "Cold, Cold Heart" ~ Tony Bennett 1951

3) "Cry" ~ Johnny Ray 1951

4) "Goodnight, Irene" ~ The Weavers 1950

5) "Harbor Lights" ~ Sammy Kaye and His Orchestra (1937 original) 1950

6) *Vaya Con Dios* ~ Les Paul and Mary Ford 1953

7) Song From *Moulin Rouge* ("Where Is Your Heart?") ~ Percy Faith and His Orchestra 1952/1953

8) "Love Letters in the Sand" ~ Pat Boone (1931 original) 1957

9) "Too Young" ~ Nat "King" Cole 1951

10) "Memories are Made of This" ~ Dean Martin 1956

11) "You Belong to Me" ~ Jo Stafford 1952

12) "Autumn Leaves" ~ Roger Williams (1945 original) 1955

13) "Goodnight, Sweetheart, Goodnight" ~ The Spaniels 1954

14) "It's Only Make Believe" ~ Conway Twitty 1958

15) "Singing the Blues" ~ Guy Mitchell 1956

16) "I Only Have Eyes for You" ~ The Flamigos (1934 original) 1959

17) "Rock and Roll Waltz" ~ Kay Starr 1955

1950s Rock and Roll

1) "Tutti Frutti" ~ Little Richard 1955

2) "Good Golly Miss Molly" ~ Little Richard 1958

3) "Be Bop-A-Lula" ~ Gene Vincent 1956

4) "Little Darlin'" ~ The Diamonds 1957

5) "Whole Lotta Shakin'" ~ Jerry Lee Lewis

6) "All Shook Up" ~ Elvis Presley 1957

7) "At the Hop" ~ Danny and the Juniors 1957

8) "Rock and Roll Music" ~ Chuck Berry 1957

9) "Rock and Roll is Here to Stay" ~ Danny and the Juniors 1958

10) "R-O-C-K" ~ Bill Haley and His Comets 1956

11) "That'll Be the Day" ~ Buddy Holly 1958

12) "Blueberry Hill" ~ Fats Domino 1956

13) "Keep a Knockin'" ~ Little Richard 1957

14) "Blue Suede Shoes" ~ Elvis Presley 1956

15) "Bo Diddley" ~ Bo Diddley 1955

16) "C'mon Everybody" ~ Eddie Cochran 1958

17) "Let the Good Times Roll" ~ Shirley and Lee 1956

18) "In the Still of the Night" ~ The Five Satins 1956

19) "Put Your Head On My Shoulder" ~ Paul Anka 1959

20) "Only You" ~ The Platters 1955

21) "Fever" ~ Little Willie John 1956

22) "See You Later, Alligator" ~ Bill Haley and His Comets 1955

23) "What'd I Say" ~ Ray Charles 1959

24) "Great Balls of Fire" ~ Jerry Lee Lewis 1957

25) "The Stroll" ~ The Diamonds 1957

Broadway Musicals

1) "Give My Regards to Broadway"
2) "Lullaby of Broadway"
3) "There's No Business Like Show Business" (*Annie Get Your Gun*) 1946
4) "Hello, Dolly!" (*Hello, Dolly!*) 1964
5) "Oklahoma!" (*Oklahoma!*) 1943
6) "Anything You Can Do" (*Annie Get Your Gun*) 1946
7) "I'm Gonna Wash That Man Right Outa My Hair" (*South Pacific*) 1949
8) "A Bushel and a Peck" (*Guys and Dolls*) 1950
9) "I Whistle A Happy Tune" (*The King and I*) 1951
10) "Shall We Dance?" (*The King and I*) 1951
11) "The Rain in Spain" (*My Fair Lady*) 1956
12) "Wouldn't it be Loverly" (*My Fair Lady*) 1956
13) "Till There was You" (*The Music Man*) 1957
14) "Seventy-Six Trombones" (*The Music Man*) 1957
15) "America" (*West Side Story*) 1957
16) "I Feel Pretty" (*West Side Story*) 1957
17) "Maria" (*West Side Story*) 1957
18) "Somewhere" (*West Side Story*) 1957
19) "The Sound of Music" (*The Sound of Music*) 1959
20) "The Lonely Goatherd" (*The Sound of Music*) 1959
21) "Consider Yourself" (*Oliver!*) 1963
22) "Matchmaker, Matchmaker" (*Fiddler on the Roof*) 1964
23) "Sunrise, Sunset" (*Fiddler on the Roof*) 1964
24) "To Life" (*Fiddler on the Roof*) 1964

Relaxation/Stretching Disk One

1) *Serenade* ~ Schubert

2) *Pavane Op. 50* ~ Faure

3) *Pavane for a Dead Princess* ~ Ravel

4) *Vocalise Op. 34* ~ Rachmaninov

5) *Oboe Concerto in D Minor Mov. 2* ~ Marcello

6) *Adagio in G Minor for Strings and Organ* ~ Albinoni

7) *Air on the G String* ~ Bach

8) *Guitar Concerto in D Major (Largo)* ~ Vivaldi

9) *Adagio for Strings* ~ Barber

10) *Concerto de Aranjuez Mov. 2* ~ Joaquin Rodrigo

Relaxation/Stretching Disk Two

1) "Raindrop" *Prelude Op. 28 No. 15* ~ Chopin

2) *Prelude Op. 28 No. 4* ~ Chopin

3) *Nocturne No. 19 Opus 72 No. 1* ~ Chopin

4) *Nocturne No. 2 Opus 9 No. 2* ~ Chopin

5) "Meditation" ~ Thais

6) "Song of India" ~ Rimsky-Korsakov

7) "The Swan" ~ Saint-Saens

8) *Gymnopedie No. 1* ~ Erik Satie

9) *The Four Seasons* (Winter) Largo ~ Vivaldi

10) "Ave Maria" ~ Bach (performed by James Galway)

11) "Arioso" ~ Bach

12) "Love's Dream After the Ball" ~ *Czibulka* (performed by London Symphony Orchestra)

13) *Concerto Andaluz* (Adagio) ~ Joaquin Rodrigo

Relaxation/Stretching Disk Three

1) "Watermark" ~ Enya

2) "Evening Falls" ~ Enya

3) "Exile" ~ Enya"

4) *"Na Laetha Geal M'oige"* ~ Enya

5) "On Your Shore" ~ Enya

6) "Miss Clare Remembers" ~ Enya

7) "Memory" from *Cats* ~ Performed by James Galway

8) "Shenandoah" ~ Performed by James Galway

9) "Over the Sea to Skye" ~ Performed by James Galway

10) "Song of the Seashore" ~ Performed by James Galway

11) "The Grand Finale" ~ Edward Scissorhands Sountrack

12) "Grand Plies" ~ Aly Tejas

13) "Plies, Flowing 6/8" ~ Bill Brown and Finis Jhung

14) "Slow Tendu 4/4, The Strager"~ Lisa Harris

15) "Tacoma Trailer" ~ Leonard Cohen

16) "Love Theme" from *Romeo and Juliet* ~ Henry Mancini

ABOUT THE AUTHOR

Meredith Faith Hamons is a board certified music therapist and the founder of North Austin Music Therapy. Her company focuses on providing services to seniors, clients with developmental disabilities, and preschoolers.

Meredith attended Duquesne University in Pittsburgh, Pennsylvania and completed her internship at the San Antonio State Hospital in San Antonio, Texas. She received additional training in neurologic music therapy from the Center for Biomedical Research in Music at Colorado State University. Meredith has been passionate about working with the elderly since she was in high school and was thrilled to create and develop a program for seniors as the foundation of her company. In addition to her clinical work, Meredith also speaks frequently on the subject of music therapy at state and national conferences.

Meredith lives in Texas with her husband and beautiful daughter. When she is not practicing music therapy, her favorite place to be is at the beach with her family.

Made in the USA
San Bernardino, CA
03 August 2015